AF560716

# DAIRYING AND RURAL DEVELOPMENT

# DAIRYING
# AND
# RURAL DEVELOPMENT

*By*

**Dr. C.R Das**

*Research Supervisor*
*Nabakrishna Choudhury Centre for*
*Development Studies*
*NALCO Square*
*Bhubaneswar, (Orissa)*

**DISCOVERY PUBLISHING HOUSE PVT. LTD.**
**NEW DELHI-110 002**

First Published – 2010

Reprinted – 2024

ISBN: 978-81-8356-608-7



**Dairying and Rural Development**

*Published by:*

**DISCOVERY PUBLISHING HOUSE**

4383/4B, Ansari Road, Darya Ganj
New Delhi-110 002 (India)
*Phone*: +91-11-23279245; 23253475; 43596065
*Mobile*: +91 9811179893 / +91 9871656464
*E-mail*: discoverybooksindia@gmail.com
orderdphbooks@gmail.com
*web*: www.discoverypublishinggroup.com

*Printed at:*
Infinity Imaging Systems
Delhi

# Acknowledgements

I place on record my humble deference to Prof (Dr) Trilochan Satapathy, Retired President of State Selection Board for encouraging me to write a book on Dairying and Rural Development. I acknowledge Prof Baidyanath Mishra, Prof L.K. Mohapatro, Prof G.C. Kar for their learned suggestions and inspiration to materialise the present study.

Equally, I acknowledge my sincere gratitude to Prof S.N. Tripathy, Gokhle Institute of Politics and Economics, Pune and Dr. R.K. Panda, Faculty in Economics of ICFAI National College, Berhampur for his kind gesture and comments on the work.

I reveal my gratitude to Dr Sujit Mishra, Indira Gandhi Institute of Development Research, Mumbai for his moral support and inspiration all through the completion of the study.

Needless to say that the success of the study deserved the help and cooperation of my family members.

I thank to my wife Reena, my son Ansuman and daughter Poonam for their selfless support.

**C.R. DAS**

# List of Abbreviations

| | | |
|---|---|---|
| ADAPT | : | Area Development Approach for Poverty Termination |
| AFC | : | Average Age at First Calving |
| AI | : | Artificial Insemination |
| AMUL | : | Anand Milk Producers Cooperative Union Ltd. |
| APL | : | Above Poverty Line |
| BPL | : | Below Poverty Line |
| CB cows | : | Cross-bred Cows |
| CB | : | Commercial Banks |
| DAHVs | : | Directorate of Animal Husbandry and Veterinary Services |
| DDP | : | Desert Development Programme |
| DDP | : | District Domestic Product |
| DPAP | : | Drought Prone Area(s) Programme |
| EEC | : | European Economic Cooperation |
| FAO | : | United Nations Food and Agriculture Organisation |
| FARD | : | Fisheries and Animal Resources Development Department |
| GOI | : | Government of India |
| GOO | : | Government of Orissa |
| ha | : | Hectares |

| | | |
|---|---|---|
| IDC | : | Indian Dairy Corporation |
| IMR | : | Infant Mortality Rate |
| IRDP | : | Integrated Rural Development Programme |
| LACs | : | Livestock Assistance Centres |
| LF | : | Large Farmers |
| LL | : | Landless |
| MF | : | Marginal Farmers |
| MFAL | : | Marginal Farmers and Agricultural Labourers Development Agency |
| MPCE | : | Monthly Per Capita Consumption Expenditure |
| MT | : | Million Tonnes |
| MVP | : | Marginal Value Productivity |
| NDDB | : | National Dairy Development Board |
| NSS | : | National Sample Survey |
| OF | : | Operation Flood |
| OMFED | : | The Orissa State Cooperative Milk-producers Federation Limited |
| PCPDC | : | Per Capita Per Day Consumption |
| RRB | : | Regional Rural Bank |
| SF | : | Small Farmers |
| SFDA | : | Small Farmers Development Agency |
| SHGs | : | Self-help Groups |
| UGS | : | Utkal Gomangal Samiti |
| UNICEF | : | United Nations International Children's Emergency Fund |

# CONTENTS

*Acknowledgements*

*List of Abbreviations*

1. **Introduction** 1
2. **Review of Literature** 20
3. **Dairy Development in Orissa** 40
4. **Profile of the Study Area** 65
5. **Economics of Dairying among Sample Households** 84
6. **Socio-economic Status of the Sample Households** 118
7. **Impact of Dairying on Rural Development** 144
8. **Summary and Conclusion** 157

*Bibliography* 182

*Index* 191

# 1

# Introduction

## BACKGROUND

In early 1999, the United Nations Food and Agriculture Organisation (FAO) declared India as the world's largest producer of milk. According to FAO's Global Food Outlook Report, Milk production in India crossed 74 million tonnes (mtby March 1999, while milk production in the U.S.A., the 'second largest producer was 71 mts (FAO, 1999). This was truly a moment of glory for India, which, less than four decades earlier, had been a milk deficit country. By 2003 milk production in India had increased to 88.1 million tonnes (NDDB, 2003). Today, the dairy movement in India continues to be unparallel in the world in terms of its scale and scope. Under Operation Flood Programme there are 170 milk unions operating over 338 districts, covering, 1,08574 village level societies and is owned by nearly 13 million farmer members and per capita availability of milk is 231 grams per day as against 112 grams per day in 1968-69 (GOI 2004).

In 1997, there were 101 million milch animals with 58 per cent cows and 42 per cent buffaloes. Over time there has been a continuous increase in the number of dairy animals, cows as well as buffaloes. Between 1982 and 1997 the population of milch cows increased from 52.5 to 58.2 millions and that of milch buffaloes from 30 to 42.7 millions. The annual rate of increase in milch cows was about one per cent during 1982-92 and 0.2 per cent during 1992-97. The rate of increase was higher in milch buffaloes both during 1980s and 1990s. An important feature emerging from dynamics of dairy population is that the milch stock of both cows and buffaloes has grown faster than the non-milch stock and implies that dairying is now practiced more for milk production (Delgodo *et al.*, 1999).

The buffalo and the cow and to a very limited extent the goat are the main milch animals in the Indian sub-continent. The buffalo contributes some 64 per cent, the cow 33 per cent and the goat 3 per cent of the total milk produced in India. India has the largest milch animal population in the world. Milk of the camel, sheep and yak is used in some parts of the region (GOI, 2001).

Like nearly all developing countries, India exhibits coexisting "organized" and "unorganized" sectors for the marketing of milk and dairy products. Sometimes called the "informal" sector, the unorganized sector may be more usefully thought of as the traditional milk market sector, comprising the marketing of raw milk and traditional products such as locally manufactured ghee, fresh cheese, and sweets. The organized or formal sector is relatively new in historical terms, and consists of western-style dairy processing based on pasteurization (Baviskar, 1993).

Dairying in India is overwhelmingly a rural activity in India and practiced by millions of small-holders as a part of mixed faming systems, wherein households combine crops and animal husbandry. In such a system dairy animals, besides generating food for household consumption, provide draught power (for cultivation of crops and transportation of goods and services) and dung as manure and fuel while sustaining on crop residues and by-products. This synergy between crops and animals not only sustains household food security but also contributes to the sustainability of the agricultural production system and environment conservation by substituting the non-renewable chemical energy use in crop production (Apte, 1993).

Small-holders, defined as the households possessing less than 2 ha of land, dominate Indian agriculture. They comprise about over 62 per cent of the rural households and own 34 per cent of the arable land. Among these households with less than 1.0 ha of land (marginal households) are predominant comprising 48 per cent of the total rural households. Another deprived category of rural households is that of landless households that constitutes about 22 per cent. Due to small land-holding size they depend on milch animals for generating livelihood (Srivastav, 1989).

Dairy production system in India mainly consists of small-holder producers. Around 100 million milch animals are spread over 5 lakh villages among 70 million farmers. There are about 100,000 village milk cooperatives with 11 million farmers as members. Landless, small and marginal farmers own 68% of milch animals and contribute nearly 62% of total milk produced. Around 63% of the available animal protein in Indian diet (10g per caput per day against a world average of 25 g) comes from milk (GOI, 2001).

Dairy production system however is undergoing a change owing to several economic and technological forces. With technological progress in agriculture and improvements in economic conditions in rural areas the non-food functions of animals are declining in importance. Animals now are viewed more as a source of food and nutrition. The demand for animal-based foods has been increasing fast due to increase in per capita income and rise in urbanization. These forces have given a commercialization orientation to dairy production. Besides, the dairy production is under economic pressure to augment income of the producers particularly small landholders for whom crop production alone cannot provide a sustainable livelihood because of increasing sub-division of land holdings.

Livestock accounts for about a quarter of the value of agricultural sector output in India, with milk accounting for bulk of it. In 1998-2000 milk accounted for 69.3 per cent of the livestock sector output. In fact, milk with a share of 18 per cent in gross value of agricultural sector has emerged as the largest agricultural commodity produced in the country.

The share of milk in livestock sector output has been rising; it increased from 68.1 per cent in 1980-82 to 69.3 per cent in 1998-2000. This shows rising importance of dairying in India. It is also an important source of employment for the rural poor. In 1983 livestock sector engaged 12 million workers (on usual activity status basis). These comprised 6.7 per cent of the total workers engaged in agricultural sector. Labour force engaged in the livestock sector has however declined marginally. In 1999-2000 livestock engaged 4.4 per cent of the total workers in the agricultural sector. One of the reasons for decline in employment in livestock sector is that over time there has been a gradual shift in dairy production systems from grazing to stall-feeding (GOI 2001).

Milk production in India, world's largest producer, is projected to go up to 108 million tonne next year from an estimated 105 MT this fiscal, according to the US Department of Agriculture (USDA). In its latest report on India s Dairy and Dairy Products, the USDA said: "Strong farm-gate prices along with rising domestic demand for a variety of milk products, supported by growth of the Indian economy, are the primary factors driving increased production". USDA added, Punjab, Karnataka, Gujarat and Andhra Pradesh are giving special emphasis to cross-breed cow development programmes leading to improvement in the milk productivity rate in these states. It also highlighted that the average performance rates of cross-bred animals - mostly local breeds with Holstein Friesian - in Punjab are quite encouraging as milk yield is 40-55 litres per dairy animal per day. Around 70-75 per cent of the indigenous cattle and buffalo population cannot be categorised under any well- defined breed or are nondescript and their milk yield levels are much lower than that of pure dairy breeds available in the country (PTI, 2008).

India's non-fat dry milk (NFDM) powder production is likely to increase by seven per cent to 370,000 tonnes in 2009-10 primarily due to increased demand for reconstituted milk during the lean production season. Butter production is forecast up by 10 per cent at 4.06 million tonne because of growing domestic demand and the greater purchasing power of the average Indian consumer (PTI, 2008).

India's milk production is expected to increase by 3.9 per cent in manufacturing year 2010-11 (US Government report, 2009).

## DAIRY AND RURAL DEVELOPMENT

In India about 76.69 per cent of the population live in rural areas. Majority of them are either cultivators or agricultural labourers. Very often they are unemployed or under employed due to vagaries of nature. The produce on the marginal lands often falls short of the dietary requirement of the farmer's household and seldom makes him indebted. Due to seasonal agricultural activity, the agricultural labourers are forced to remain unemployed and starve for want of alternative source of livelihood. The agricultural labourers are paid at the minimum rate which is not sufficient even to meet the minimum day to day requirements. As a result substantial section of the rural workforce lives in a state of utter poverty. An effective employment policy is the most appropriate instrument for achieving this goal with the framework of the existing economic and political system.

A substantial proportion of the rural workers are self employed. Females prove a large part of the unpaid family organisational behaviour in agriculture and the proportion of women and children in the labour force tends to be higher than in other sectors. The participation rate of females as cultivators in creased from 3.6 per cent in 1971 to 4.65 per cent in 1981 and the participation of females as agricultural labours increased from 6.13 per cent to 6.46 per cent during the same period.

Dairying is a significant source of generating rural income and employment. It provides supplementary income to the farmer households and utilises the idle family members available in the farmers families. Farmers usually get income at the time of crop harvest once or twice in a year. Farmers usually incur expenditure for various farm operation through out the period of plant growth. Due to lack of alternative source of regular income, they are often indebted to meet the necessary farm expenditure. Instead, income from milk is regular so that the farmers take the advantage of utilising the money from milk for the farm. So, dairying is mostly practised as a subsidiary industry to agriculture. Dairying provides much more stable and continuous economic based than crop production and security against the vicissitudes of drought and famine.

Dairy development programmes are labour intensive, having favourable cost-benefit ratio and are particularly suitable for the weaker sections of the rural community, and have got redistribution effect in favour of them. As cattle and buffalo raising involves intensive use of labour usually, more than many other enterprises, it offers more employment and income opportunities to small and marginal farmers and agricultural labourers. A very large proportion of the female labour force finds scope for fuller utilisation in several operations connected with cattle and buffalo rearing.

Dairying apart from generating substantial direct employment, has also a large built-in potential for generating indirect employment in several ancillary activities like manufacture of feed for livestock, milk processing, and manufacture of milk products, etc. besides generating rural income and employment, milk protects human health by supplying rich proteins and nutrients and helps increase the standard of living of the rural masses. The milch animals also provide rich manure for the farmer to raise farm productivity.

A well organised dairy industry helps to increase milk production in rural areas by introducing of high-yielding breeds of cattle, and of better feeding and management practices. Enhancing the production resulting in better income levels to the rural population. Priority is sought to be given to the dairy industry because of the impact it has on the economy of the small and marginal farmers and agricultural labourers by way of generating larger employment opportunities and thus helping to increase their incomes.

It is well-known fact that the Indian agriculture faces the problem of disguised unemployment and the resultant problem of poverty and inequality of income distribution. Hence, the supreme task of planning is to drain this labour reservoir by creating employment opportunities and by channelling the employed and underemployed into productivity works. Dairy farming serves this purpose.

Dairy farming can also absorb large number of agricultural labourers, and rural poor and it provides large scale employment opportunities throughout the year. This subsidiary occupation in playing a vital role in improving the rural economy which is mainly agriculture based. The advantage of the dairy industry is that the gestation period is very short and the benefit of development activities can be enjoyed very soon.

## THE HISTORY OF DAIRY DEVELOPMENT IN INDIA

The history of the dairy development can be broadly classified into two distinct phases: pre- and post-Operation Flood. It is because Operation flood is considered to be central-event of twentieth century dairying in India.

### Dairying Prior to Operation Flood

The earliest attempts at dairy development can be traced back to British rule, when the Defence Department established military dairy farms to ensure the supply of milk and butter to the colonial army. The first of these farms was set up in Allahabad in 1913; subsequent facilities were established at Bangalore, Ootacamund and Kamal. These farms were well maintained and, even in the early stages, improved milch animals were raised. As animals were reared under farm conditions, some herd improvement was made using artificial insemination. This approach did not have any impact on the supply of milk to urban consumers, which was of major concern to civilian authorities but less important to the military (Huria and Acharya, 1980).

With the growth of the population in urban areas, consumers had to depend on milk vendors who kept cattle in these areas and sold their milk, often door-to-door. As a result, several cattle sheds came into existence in different cities. This was not an environmentally sound approach. As the main objective of the milk vendors was to maximize profit, they started increasing the lactation period by using the focus system. In the process, these high-yielding cattle developed sterility problems, which considerably reduced the number of calvings. Once the cattle became unproductive, they were sold to slaughterhouses. This practice systematically drained the country of its genetically superior breeds (*ibid.*).

To some extent, the World War II gave impetus to private dairies with modestly modernized processing facilities. In the cities of Mumbai, Kolkata, Chennaiand Delhi, and even in some large townships, processed milk, table butter and ice-cream were available, though not on a large scale. Polsons, Keventers and the Express Dairy were some of the pioneer urban processing dairies. These dairies were not concerned with improving the breed of milch animals reared in rural pockets but instead were content with contracting milk supplies through middlemen or their own staff. Milk producers as well as consumers were exploited. These early modem systems did not bring about significant shifts in milk production, nor did they develop quality milch animals. To a large extent, despite modernized processing facilities, dairying remained unorganized (*ibid.*).

With the initiation of India's First Five-year Plan in 1951, modernization of the dairy industry became a priority for the government. Initial government action in this regard consisted of organizing "milk schemes" in large cities. To stimulate milk production, the government implemented the Integrated Cattle Development Project (ICDP) and the Key Village Scheme (KVS), among other similar programmes. In the absence of a stable and remunerative market for milk producers, however, milk production remained more or less stagnant. During the two decades between 1951 and 1970, the growth rate in milk production was barely 1 per cent per annum (*ibid.*).

During the 1960s, various State governments tried out different strategies to develop dairying, including establishing dairies run by their own departments, setting up cattle colonies in urban areas and organizing milk schemes. Almost invariably, dairy processing plants were built in cities rather than in the milk sheds where milk was produced. This urban orientation to milk production led to the establishment of cattle colonies in Bombay, Calcutta, and Madras. These government projects had extreme difficulties in organizing rural milk procurement and running milk schemes economically, yet none concentrated on creating an organized system for procurement of milk, which was left to contractors and middlemen. As the government dairies were meeting barely one-third of the urban demand, the queues of consumers became longer while the rural milk producer was left in the clutches of the trader and the moneylender. Thus, milk procurement from the urban areas was the major problem in Indian dairying.

## Amul and the Evolution of the Anand Model

Polsons - a private dairy at Anand - procured milk from milk producers through middlemen, processed it and then sent the milk to Bombay, some 425 km away (Korten, 1981). Bombay was a good market for milk and Polsons profited immensely. In the mid-1940s, when the milk producers in Kaira asked for a proportionate share of the trade margins, they were denied. The milk producers went on strike, refusing to supply milk to Polsons. On the advice of Sardar Vallabhbhai Patel, a leader in India's independence movement, the milk producers registered the Kaira District Cooperative Milk Producers' Union, now popularly known as AMUL, in 1946. The Kaira union procured milk from affiliated village-level milk societies. This was the genesis of organized milk marketing in India, a pioneering effort that opened a new vista for dairy development in the country (Gupta, 1987).

Between 1946 and 1952, AMUL's policy was directed towards obtaining monopoly rights for the sale of milk to the Bombay milk scheme. In 1952, it succeeded in achieving its purpose after the Government of Bombay cancelled the contract with Polsons and handed over the entire business of supplying milk from the Kaira district to AMUL. However, as the Bombay milk scheme was committed to purchasing all the milk produced by the Aarey Milk Colony in Bombay, it had not taken AMUL's milk during the peak winter months. The disposal of this surplus milk posed difficulties for AMUL, forcing it to cut down on purchases from its member societies, which affected members' confidence. In this background Amul decided to produce milk products like butter, *ghee* and milk powder by installing a new dairy plant in 1955 the aid from United Nations Children's Fund (UNICEF) (Dogra, 1985).

## OPERATIONS FLOOD

The strategy for organized dairy development in India was actually conceived in the late 1960s, within a few years after the National Dairy Development Board (NDDB) was founded in 1965.

In October 1964, on the occasion of the inauguration of AMUL's cattle feed plant, the then Prime Minister of India, Lal Bahadur Shastri, spent the night as the guest of a village milk cooperative society near Anand. Impressed by the socio-economic changes brought about by the milk cooperatives, he expressed the desire for a national-level organization to replicate Anand Model dairy cooperatives throughout the country and to make available multi-disciplinary, professional dairy expertise to dairies in the public and cooperative sectors. Thus, in 1965, NDDB was registered under the Societies Registration Act, the Charitable Trust Act and the Public Trust Act and headquarters were established at Anand.

During its initial stages, NDDB was assisted financially by the Government of India, the Danish Government and by AMUL. It also received aid from the United Nations International Children's Emergency Fund (UNICEF) in the form of teaching material and equipment.

In 1969, when the Government of India approved the Operation Flood programme and its financing through the monetization of World Food Programme-gifted commodities, it was found that the statutes under which NDDB was registered did not provide for handling of government funds. Therefore, in 1970 the government established a public-sector company, the Indian Dairy Corporation (IDC). The IDC was given responsibility for receiving the project's donated commodities; testing their quality; their storage and transfer to user dairies; and receiving the dairies' payments. Thus, it served as a finance-cum-promotion entity while the entire Operation Flood technical support was provided by NDDB (*ibid.*).

To avoid any duplication in their activities or overlap of functions, the IDC and NDDB were eventually merged into a newly constituted NDDB by an Act of Parliament passed in October 1987. The Act designated the NDDB as an institution of national importance (*ibid.*).

Launched in 1970, Operation Flood has helped dairy farmers direct their own development, placing control of the resources they create in their own hands. The bedrock of Operation Flood has been village milk producers' cooperatives, which procure milk and provide inputs and services, making modern management and technology available to members. Operation Flood's objectives include Increase milk production ("a flood of milk"), augment rural incomes, fair prices for consumers.

### *Phase I (1970-1980)*

Phase I was financed by the sale of skimmed milk powder and butter oil gifted by the European Union through the World Food Programme. During its first phase, Operation Flood linked 18 of India's premier milksheds with consumers in India's four major metropolitan cities: Delhi, Mumbai, Calcutta and Madras.

### *Phase II (1981-85)*

Phase II increased the milk sheds from 18 to 136; 290 urban markets expanded the outlets for milk. By the end of 1985, a self-sustaining system of 43,000 village cooperatives covering 4.25 million milk producers had become a reality. Domestic milk powder production increased from 22,000 tons in the pre-project year to 140,000 tons by 1989.

### *Phase III (1985-1996)*

Phase III enabled dairy cooperatives to expand and strengthen the infrastructure required to procure and market increasing volumes of milk. Operation Flood's Phase III consolidated India's dairy cooperative movement, adding 30,000 new dairy cooperatives to the 42,000 existing societies organized during Phase II. Increased emphasis to research and development in animal health and animal nutrition.

Operation Flood was conceived and implemented as much more than a dairy programme. Rather, dairying was seen as an instrument of development, generating employment and regular incomes for millions of rural people. "Operation Flood can be viewed as a twenty year experiment confirming the Rural Development Vision" (World Bank, 1999).

## THE PROBLEM AND ITS SETTING

In view of India's consistently deficient in milk production by more than 30 per cent to meet its minimum standards of nutritional requirement, various measures were taken to narrow the gap between the demand for the supply of milk in the country sine the second half of the sixties. There after daily activity spread very fast in the rural areas of many states, especially in Gujarat. This led to an increase in the production and productivity of milk in the country. However, so far as Orissa is concerned, although it is about 4.4 per cent of the total milch animal population of the country, yet milk production of the State amounts to only 0.84 per cent of total milk output of India. In respect of consumption of milk, the per capita availability in the State is meagre substantially below the national average. In view of this, the imperative need for an intensive dairy development in the State hardly needs any emphasis. What is more important is that, dairy development has significantly crucial role to play as a poverty alleviation measure in the rural areas of Orissa. The programme currently implemented as operation flood, is envisaged to improve the socio-economic conditions of the milk producers, particularly those belonging to the economically disadvantaged groups, such as, the landless labourers, the small and the marginal farmers, the Scheduled Caste and Scheduled tribes.

However, it is distressing to observe that despite beneficial economic potentials and the investment made thereon with a number of incentives offered to the milk producer by the government, the pace of development of commercial dairying, particularly in the rural areas of Orissa has not at all been encouraging. Naturally, therefore, there are serious lacunae in the formation and execution of dairy development programmes in the state. Thus, it would by highly rewarding to locate and identify the different shortfalls on this front and offer certain valuable guidelines that can improve the state of affairs. This requires an in-depth and comprehensive analysis of the entire gamut of dairy development process in Orissa.

## THE OBJECTIVES OF THE STUDY

Against such a backdrop the objectives of the present study are:

(a) to evaluate the nature, magnitude and dimension of dairy development in Orissa;

(b) to find out to what extent has the dairy farming been instrument of economic and social change in the state, particularly in the rural sector, with special reference to the generation of the volume of additional employment and income, with dairying as primary as well as a subsidiary occupation not the adaptors;

(c) To analyse the milk production functions, i.e. to estimate a realistic functional relationship relating to production, processing and marketing of milk in the state with particular reference to, production costs incurred by the milk producers, the price received by the dairy owners, the procurement processing and marketing costs, the selling price or the price paid by the consumers and the share of the middlemen operating in the line;

(d) To examine the pattern of ownership of dairy animals in the rural sector and the distribution of productivity among the different categories of farmers according to size class of holding in order to find out as to whether the operation flood programme has benefited the actually intended dairy-household or not;

(e) To highlight the different major socio-economic constraints operating rapid dairy development, such as, the issues of quality and quantity of animal feed, communal grazing grounds, cross breed cows or indigenous cows, government support in the form of finance, veterinary and management regimes warranted for farming including the organisation of dairy cooperative.

## HYPOTHESIS OF THE STUDY

The major hypotheses developed in the course of the study and put to empirical test are:

(a) Dairy sector in Orissa enjoys the potential to contribute significantly to income and employment generation;

(b) Dairying generates part-time employment without coming into conflict with any other full time economic pursuit and thereby creates supplementary income.

(c) For weaker section, with limited alternative income earning opportunity, income from dairy enterprise can be crucial for their livelihood and may constitute the single largest source.

(d) By and large, the intermediary agencies in milk marketing appropriate a significant percentage of the selling price paid by the consumers;

(e) Incremental income from dairy can improve with maintenance of higher yielding cross-breed cows by farmers, governmental support in the form of animal health care, community grazing ground, improvement of the existing marketing system and provision of remunerative prices to the milk producers.

## STUDY APPROACH AND METHODOLOGY

In order to assess the impact of dairying on rural development, efforts are made to collect data from dairy and non-dairy households. For the purpose of drawing samples, two coastal districts i.e. Puri and Ganjam having high potential in dairying are selected purposively for analysing the impact of dairying. Different selected indicators of dairy households are compared with the corresponding values of the non-dairy households with a view to arrive at the changes arising due to dairying. Keeping in view the objectives of the study, present study is mostly based on primary data. However, secondary data are also used to highlight the macro performance of dairy sector in India in general and Orissa in particular. The study analyses the impact of dairy development on rural development considering primary data obtained from 200 households of 4 villages under 2 blocks in Ganjam district and 180 households of four villages under 2 blocks in Puri District. The details of selection of the districts, blocks and households are as follows:

### Selection of Districts

Two coastal districts - Puri and Ganjam - in view of its high potential in dairy sector are purposefully selected.

### Selection of Blocks and Villages

In each selected districts, two blocks are purposefully selected considering the distance form the district head quarters. In the selection procedure, one block lying close to district headquarters and one block lying distance from the district headquarters are considered. In Puri district, Satyabadi a nearby block to the district headquarters and Kanas relatively distant are considered. Similarly in Ganjam district, Rangeilunda, a nearer block to district headquarters situated at Konisi and Surada a relatively distant block from the district headquarters are chosen.

On the basis of simple random sampling, using Random Number Tables, from the list of census villages two villages from each selected block are considered. The selected villages from each block are shown in Table 1.1.

**Table 1.1 : List of Villages Selected in the Study**

| Districts | Blocks | Villages (GPs) |
|---|---|---|
| Puri | Kanas | Trilochanpur, Jankia |
| | Nimapara | Denuan, Jageswarpur |
| | | Rangeilunda, |
| Ganjam | Rangeilunda (Konisi) | Durabahadurpeta |
| | Surada | Amrutulu and Gopalpur Sasan |

## Selection of Respondents

From the selected eight villages in all the blocks, in total 200 dairying households this rate of 25 households from each selected village is selected. In Ganjam of the total 200 sample households, 100 households are engaged in dairy activity and he rest 100 households are non-dairy households. The immediate neighbour of the dairy household is considered. If the adjacent household of the dairy household is again a dairy household, the next adjacent household are considered. In Puri, 100 dairying households and 80 non-dairy households selected for the purpose of the study. So total 380 households surveyed through pre tested schedule questionnaire designed for the study.

## Definitions used in the Study

For the purpose of this study, the following definitions have been used:

- *Dairy and non-dairy households*

For the purpose of the study, the households having milch animals and involved in dairying activities during reference

**Table 1.2 : Selection of Respondents**

| Sl No. | Particulars | Ganjam | | | | Puri | | | |
|---|---|---|---|---|---|---|---|---|---|
| | | Konisi | | Suruda | | Nimapada | | Kanas | |
| | | Dura-Bahadurpeta | Range-lunda | Amrutulu | Gopalpur Sasan | Denuan | Jageswar | Jankia | Trilo-chanpur |
| 1. | Tota; Households | 518 | 298 | 312 | 208 | 614 | 118 | 212 | 176 |
| 2. | Dairy Households | 216 | 118 | 113 | 88 | 331 | 77 | 109 | 95 |
| 3. | Sample Diary Households | 25 | 25 | 25 | 25 | 25 | 25 | 25 | 25 |
| 4. | Sample Non-Diary Households | 25 | 25 | 25 | 25 | 20 | 20 | 20 | 20 |

year 2003-04 which is a normal year are defined as dairying households. Whereas, households having only adult male cattle or young stocks or not undertaking dairying activities are classified as non-dairying households.

- *Dairying*

'Dairying is used to denote all type of dairy activities such as rearing dairy animals especially cattle and buffaloes, production, processing and marketing of milk and milk products simultaneously. On the other hand, if these activities are not simultaneously carried out have been viewed as non-dairying.

## Reference Period

The reference period is from 1st March 2003-31st April 2004 during which time the field study was carried out and the period was a normal one from the agricultural point of view. For analysing the socio economy pattern of dairying, type of production, consumption, marketing, income, expenditure, impact of dairying etc., and the corresponding values for this period was considered.

## Scheme of the Study

The objectives of presenting the results of the study are sought through eight relevant chapters. Chapter 1 deals with the background and history of dairy development in India. Besides the objectives, hypotheses and methodology are outlined in this chapter. Review of the existing literature on dairying is presented in Chapter 2. Chapter 3 focuses on the dairy development in Orissa. Profile of the study area in terms of the selected districts, blocks and villages are highlighted in Chapter 4. The economics of dairying among the sample households are presented in Chapter 5 by analysing the primary data obtained from sample households. The socio-economic impacts of dairying among dairy households are measured in Chapter 6 by using different statistical tool.

Similarly, the impacts of dairying on rural development are explained by considering suitable indicators, which are presented in Chapter 7. Finally, the summary and conclusion of findings, observations and recommendations are presented in Chapter 8.

## Statistical Techniques Used

For analysing data in the present study, time-series analysis, mean analysis, percentage deviation methods etc. are used. For analysing the incidence food poverty calories shortfall methods are followed. In order to assess the determinants of dairying among the sample households econometric tools like linear Cobb-Douglas Production Function are estimated. For analysing the level of significance between the mean differences among dairying and non-dairying household the stat "t" test are employed.

## Statistical Tools Used

For obtaining information from among the sample households, a detailed structured questionnaire pertaining to the socio-economic activities related to dairying and the different socio-economic impacts at household level etc. has been prepared.

# 2

# Review of Literature

An attempt has been made in this chapter to focus on the development of dairy and its role in the socio-economic progress of weaker section of the society. Hence, an overview of existing literature on the subject has been made to have an insight to the problem and also to fill the research gap through the present study.

Studies conducted by eminent authors brought out by *Indian Journal of Agricultural Economics* in 1975 (July-Sept) Vol. XXX(3) provide an inner thought to scholars working in the field of dairy development.

A study conducted by Dhondyal and Singh (1965) indicates that livestock economics in UP and found that buffalo rearing on the land holding upto 6 ha was with no profit no loss; 6 to 8 ha farm there was profit and above 8 ha there was toss. They also found that production cost of cow's milk was more than its price. Their analysis revealed that buffalo is comparatively more profitable than cow, for milk production.

A study conducted by Phukan and Goshain (1975) in Brahmaputra Valley of Assam found that income from dairying was Rs. 3630 per farm while the total income (including other sources) was Rs. 4045 for the latter. Thus dairy enterprise in combination with crop enterprise appears more profitable than pure dairy enterprise.

George and Srivastava (1975) have calculated benefit cost per buffalo in Baroda district. The internal rate of return was 44 per cent of cattle development. At discount rates of 7.5 and 10 per cent, the benefit cost ratio including inputted costs came to be 1.37 and 1.36 respectively. They concluded that "dairying could be used as an effective means for increasing the income position of the rural poor if adequate finances lined with extension and marketing facilities are provided."

Amongst the sectoral unions of workers in the unorganized sector, the national level federations of building and construction workers is one of the largest in India.

D.S. Thakur's (1975) analysis on progress of milk societies, milk unions and the impact of milk co-operatives on the economic conditions of rural people including the weaker sections in the Gujarat was remarkable in terms of increasing number of milk societies; total membership, share capital, reserve fund, net profit, milk collected and transactions were made since their inception. He also examiners the impact of technical inputs disbursed by milk co-operatives on production and marketed surplus of milk, adoption of improved agricultural inputs and the annual income of the milk producers. He found that the annual income from dairy enterprise per household was Rs. 2224 against Rs. 5346 from crop enterprises the further in the villages under experimental group. The income from former was about a little less than half of the latter pointed out that. The milk production per animal and marketed surplus is a little higher in the experimental villages than that in the control villages. In experimental villages, the use of improved agricultural input and total incomes are found to be higher. The marketed surplus of milk is higher in the case of the weaker sections compared to the medium and large farmers in general seems to be too obvious a conclusion.

Pandey *et al.* (1975) evaluate the economic impact of Dairy Development Project, Aligarh, on milk production, number and composition of milk animals, area under fodder crops, incidence of diseases and the attitude and awareness of the farmers towards various dairy development programmes. During 1971-

71 to 1974-75, the buffalo population and milk production in the project villages are reported to have increased by 28 and 33 per cent respectively. He found effective control of mortality rate and incidence of diseases on cattle population. The average gross income per farm family has increased by about 10 per cent during the last five years contribution of milk production enterprise to the total farm income increased from 13 per cent in 1970-71 to 17 per cent in 1974-75, whereas income from crops is reported to be practically unchanged.

Kahlon *et al.* (1975) conducted a study in Ludhiana District of Punjab show through a linear programming exercise that there is significant potential for raising incomes of the farms through optimization of resources coupled with adoption of complete package of recommended practices and dairy husbandry. They observed that income from dairy cattle was obtained through out the year while income from crop husbandry logged by few months. According to optimal plans drawn for the existing farms having dairy enterprise, the large tractor farms yielded an increase of income of 76.82 per cent compared to 44.06 per cent increase on the small farms and 66.95 per cent increase on the medium tractor operated farms at the recommended level of technology.

Garg and Azad (1975) studied western Uttar Pradesh and found that maize, potato, wheat was the most intensive crop rotation in that locality, yielding a net return of Rs. 6,593 per hectare, compared to it, the net return from dairy enterprise was as high as Rs. 7,288 per hectare.

Radha Krishnan and Sivanandham (1975) in their research paper use of the input output for 90 farms situated in Sarkass Amkulam block of Coimbatore Taluk (Tamil Nadu) in order to explore the possibilities of maintaining the milky animals within the availability of fodder, labour and other resources. Linear programming model is used to arrive at optimum cropping and livestock combination on the average situation form. They had shown that the readjustment of cropping pattern to suit the farming situation would earn 44.21 per cent additional income and the maximum number of milk animals that a farmer can maintain would be five. The set of constraints did not include such an important resource as capital and housing arrangements for the cattle. Also, an assumption that bullock pairs are not maintained on the farm since it can be hired; would also invalidate the results of this exercise.

Raut *et al.* (1977) estimated cost of production of milk on different categories of households by utilizing the data collected in a large-scale sample survey carried out in Dhulia region of Maharashtra. He observed that the milk production cost including family labour was minimum for landless cattle owners and maximum for small farmers ranging from Rs. 1.02 to Rs. 1.35 per kg of milk, respectively.

Rao (1978) formulated the input-output relationship for crossbred cattle maintained by urban households in Kamal and fitted linear, semi-log and Cobb-Douglas types of production functions. The result showed that Holstein crossbreds gave superior performance as compared to Brown Swiss and Jersey crosses. Concentrate feed was Found to be a better source of DCP in rainy and summer seasons. The results indicated; possibilities of economic substitution of concentrate by green fodder such as *berseem* during winter season. The coefficient of order of lactation was found to be positive and significant in winter and summer seasons. In the crossbreds, the coefficients of age of first calving. The DCP from green fodder and concentrates were found to be significant. It was interesting to note that the age of first calving and market value of the cow had a significant effect on milk production during one season and negative influence in another season for the same set of crossbred cattle.

Reddy *et al* (1978) analysed data pertaining to 72 crossbred cows and 30 buffaloes to study economic allocation of feed and fodder. The cows, on an average yielded 9.29 kg milk per day and had an intake of 3.71 kg concentrates and 19.16 kg fodder, while corresponding values for buffaloes were 5.08, 2.56 and 25.44 kg, respectively. Linear, Quadratic and Cobb-Douglas production functions were applied to the data. The linear equation was the most appropriate for working out different feed combinations for specified levels of milk production. It was also used to estimate the marginal rate of substitution of fodder for concentrate. Results have shown that concentrates have a feed value for cows than for buffaloes.

Reddy and Mathur (1978) studied economic performance of crossbred cows and buffaloes on the basis of season-wise variation at Bangalore. The proportion of cattle calving in the rainy, winter and summer season was 34.72 per cent, 42.37 per cent and 22.91 per cent, respectively and the proportion of buffaloes calving was 56.67 per cent, 41.66 per cent and 1.67 per cent, respectively.

Rekib *et al* (1978) studied the cost of milk production with crossbred cows at Allahabad, Hyderabad, Jhansi, Midnapore and Poona centres of the All India Coordinated Project on economics of milk production during 1972-75. The average cost of milk production was Rs. 1.51, Rs. 1.14, Rs. 1.55, Rs. 182 and Rs. 1.77 at Allahabad, Hyderabad, Jhansi, Midnapore and Poona centres respectively. The most important components of the total cost of milk production were feed and fodder, human labour and the fixed cost, which contributed about 60 per cent, 16 per cent and 18 per cent, respectively. The feed cost was observed to be minimum at Jhansi and Hyderabad, where greater thrust was on fodder-based ration during the period. The correlation coefficients between milk yield and expenditure were 0.85, 0.84 and 0.89 in 1972-73, 1973-74 and 1974-75, respectively, indicating the high degree of interdependence between these two factors.

Singh *et al.* (1979) estimated that the cost of buffalo milk production was the lowest in the rainy season and highest in the summer season in two zones of Haryana State. For the State as a whole, the estimated cost of milk production was Rs. 1.83 per litre. The average yield of buffaloes in the State was 5.74 litres per day during the rainy season and 4.45 litres per day in summer. The study on input-output relationship revealed that the regression coefficient for age of the milch animal was negative and significant for all the seasons, whereas regression coefficients for order of lactation were obviously positive and significant in all seasons. This shows that milk yield increases with the increase in order of lactation and is contrary to the reality. The regression coefficients of the concentrates, consistently, had impressive influence on the milk yield. The production function analysis also shows that the farmers were feeding more dry fodder to buffalo in the summer season, and more green fodder in the rainy and winter seasons.

Acharya and Pawar (1980) studied the comparative economics of different breeds of cattle and buffaloes in Maharashtra and observed that the average milk production of crossbred cows was 8.68 litres per day. The total milk of crossbred cattle in lactation was estimated to be about 2609 litres. On the other hand, milk production of buffalo and local cattle in lactation was 1359 litres and 604 litres, respectively. The average milk production cost per litre of milk of a crossbred cow, buffalo and local cow was observed to be Rs. 1.60, Rs. 1.89 and Rs. 2.52, respectively. The total labour requirement of 163 days for buffalo during the inter calving period was highest as compared to 159 days for crossbred cow and 133 days for local cow. This could be attributed to the larger inter calving period among buffaloes (574 days) than cows.

Ram *et al.* (1980), in his study have explained that the economic optima were obtained at 39.9 kg of green fodder and 4.13 kg of concentrate. This would generate a profit of Rs. 6.96 per cow per day over feed cost for an estimated milk yield of 14.28 kg.

Singh, K. and Das. V.M., (1980) while conducting study on impact of operational flood at the village level found that the proportion of animals in milk to total milk animals was higher in the co-operative villages than in the control villages. The average household income from all sources was substantially higher in the co-operative villages than non-operative villages; however, the distribution of income from milk did not show any trend. The study further observed that the average employment of family labour in milk production was marketed higher in the co-operative villages than in the control villages. The awareness of scientific animal health care and improved feeding practices of respondents of co-operative village are more than control villages.

Kherde, R.L. and Subramaniom, R. (1980) Studied the impact of milk marketing through dairy co-operatives and found significant increase in the milk production in the co-operative villages whereas there was decline in the duration of age at first claving, claving interval, dry period and mortality rate in buffaloes. The net income of the milk producers increased under co-operative villages probably due to efficient and assured milk marketing through co-operatives. Employment days generated per farm in co-operative villages were more than non-eo-operative villages.

In their article Huria and Acharya (1980) examined the following issues on dairy development in India: (i) in the absence of sufficient pasture land how to reduce the cost of animal feeding by keeping energy input output ratio be kept. as favourable as possible, (ii) to preserve the symbiosis between dairying and agriculture so as to provide low cost energy system. For the better utilisation of agricultural waste small size land holding farmers should keep small number of dairy animals, (iii) from the point of view of nutrition, milk is indispensable for infants, when breast milk is for any reason lacking so it is important to workout procedures for costing milk in a realistic way, so that price always acts as a stimulus to sustained dairy development and (iv) Modern technology needs constantly to be reviewed for ideas that favour the Indian situation, such as the development of ultra high temperature (UHT) treatment of milk that stores for six months without refrigeration, or the extending of milk supplies using oilseed proteins. The important strides that dairy development has made need to be sustained through constant scholarly evaluation and mid-course corrections of direction or emphasis.

Singh (1980) worked out the economics of milk production of different breeds of milch cattle on different size of farms in Jauanpur district in Uttar Pradesh. The study revealed that the cost of maintenance of a local cow, crossbred cow, local buffaloes and graded buffaloes for the lactation period was Rs. 772, Rs. 1,485, Rs. 2,475 and Rs. 3,351, respectively. The average milk yield per day for buffalo was 4.50 litres. The milk yield of local cow and local buffalo was 1.80 litres and 3.10 litres, respectively.

The net maintenance cost per day of buffalo was, worked out to be Rs. 8.95 as against Rs. 4.60 for crossbred cow.

Pandey and Kumar (1981) applied the Cobb-Douglas type of production function to input-output data in dairy development project of Aligarh in Uttar Pradesh. The results of the study are indicative of a substantial scope for attaining higher degree of economic efficiency in milk production by raising the quality of green fodder and simultaneously reducing the quantities of dry fodder fed to the dairy animals. In the case of Jersey crosses, the effect of concentrates and green fodder on dairy productivity was positive. In terms of specification of explanatory variables, the study has the novelty of using quantities of green fodder, dry fodder and concentrates in terms of Berseem equivalents. The equivalents were computed on the basis of TDN content of feedstuffs.

Singh (1982) analysed the cost of milk production in Kamal during 1981-82 and observed that the cost of production per litre of milk was Rs. 3.24. The share of fixed cost was found to be 18 per cent of the variable expenditure. After deducting the value of the dung and the sale value of the young stock, the net cost of milk production was estimated at Rs. 3.16 per litre. The estimated cost function with cost per litre of milk as dependent variable and milk production as independent variable showed that the cost per litre of milk would decline with increase in the level of production in a herd. The optimum scale of the herd, when the cost per litre was minimum was found at 84 litres of milk output per day.

Patel's another study (1983), in rural Andhra Pradesh shows that the net cost of production of a litre of buffalo milk ranged from Rs. 1.78 to Rs. 2.41 in the districts, the overall average being Rs. 2.20. The inter seasonal comparison revealed that the cost was highest in rainy season (Rs. 2.30) followed by summer (Rs. 2.08) and winter (Rs. 1.66). With regard to the individual cost components, feed cost constituted the single biggest item of total cost (54 to 69 per cent) followed by fixed cost and labour cost. The share of concentrates in the total feed cost worked out to about one-fourth in buffaloes and one-third in crossbred cattle.

Sharma (1983) in Gwalior found a wide range of fluctuation in the feed cost between 43 per cent to 69 per cent and cost of labour between 12 per cent and 14 per cent. Rao (1986) in Andhra Pradesh studied economics of buffaloes wherein the feed cost was as high as 65 per cent. The review of earlier studies reveals that during the past five decades, there was not much fluctuation in the proportions of different cost factors of milk production in India as well. The feed cost revolved around 60 per cent on an average, except in one or two cases.

According to Singh (1984), the net cost of milk production for a litre of buffalo milk in Haryana state decreased with the increase in the size of land holding; it was observed maximum for the landless cattle owners (Rs. 204) and the minimum for the large farmers (Rs. 1.90), the average cost per litre for the state being Rs. 1.96. Season wise, it was maximum in summer season (Rs. 2.17) followed by monsoon season (Rs. 2.10) and winter season (Rs. 1.77). The overall average cost per litre of cow's milk worked out to Rs. 1.89. In order to establish the input-output relationship between the milk yield and the various explanatory variables, milk production functions were fitted. Out of all the functions tried, linear equations were finally selected, since it provided better estimates of the regression coefficients. The results for the state as a whole revealed that the stage of lactation and the human labour had highly significant and negative influence on the milk yield. As against this, the order of lactation, expenditure on green fodder, concentrates and the price of the animal bore significant and positive relationship with the milk yield. Miscellaneous recurring expenditure and the depreciation and interest on fixed assets did not appear to exercise any profound influence on the milk yield of buffaloes in the study area. In general, a rupee additional expenditure on green fodder resulted in an increase of 0.45 litres of milk yield per day. Similar increase in the case of dry fodders and concentrates resulted in an increase of 0.17 litres and 0.15 litres of milk, respectively. The investment of an additional rupee on green fodder and concentrates resulted in more than a rupee worth of milk.

Ram and Singh (1985) reported from Kamal that the net cost of maintenance during 1979-80 per cow per day of local cow, purebred exotic, crossbred cattle and buffalo was observed to be Rs. 9.74, Rs. 11.42, Rs. 13.37 and Rs. 9.91 respectively. The average yields for the respective. breeds were, found to be 5.42, 7.70, 9.76 and 4.00 litres. The net cost of producing a litre of milk after taking into account the income received from the disposal of dung worked out to Rs. 1.80, Rs. 1.48, Rs. 1.37 and Rs. 2.48 respectively. This clearly showed that though the average cost of maintenance of a crossbred cattle was 37 and 35 per cent higher than the local and graded buffaloes, the cost of production of a litre of milk in the respective breeds was 32 and 81 per cent lower. The cost of milk production was the highest for the animals yielding below 1200 litres of milk in lactation. It was observed to be lowest (Rs. 1.27) for those animals producing between 3601 to 4000 litres of milk. In the case of crossbred chattel the per day milk yield varied from 4.30 to 13.79 litres. The relative cost of producing a litre of milk was observed to be Rs. 2.73 and Rs. 1.20. In the case of buffaloes, the average yield per day varied from 2.60 to 5.50 litres. The cost of production too varied between Rs. 3.75 and Rs. 1.84.

Rao (1985) worked out the factors affecting the cost of milk production in the command area of Nagarjuna Sagar Project, during the year 1981-82. Linear and Cobb-Douglas type of production function were fitted. It was observed from the study that the inputs like green fodder and concentrates were the principal factors affecting milk *production* in alt size groups of farms. Regarding labour, only marginal farmers were utilizing this input in an efficient manner, while the rest of the farmer groups were over utilizing it and hence the component could be reduced.

Singh, M. *et al.* (1985) conducted a study on operational efficiency of U.P. milk co-operatives and found that the services like veterinary aid, cattle feed and marketing facilities were insufficient. Input services like artificial insemination (AI), pregnancy diagnosis, balance cattle feed and vaccination against communicable disease have appositive bearing on the efficiency of milk cooperatives. And concluded that the communication system should be made strong for quick transmission of latest technology, technical know-how pertaining to dairy as well as input services should be strengthened in the state to attain desired efficiency of milk co-operative societies.

Singh and Singh (1986) estimated the economic performance of buffaloes in different seasons for the year 1981-82 in Chaka Block of Allahabad District (UP.). It was observed that on an average, per day maintenance cost varied from Rs. 8.22 to Rs. 11.43 on different size of farms and in different seasons. The average milk yield of a milch buffalo was observed to be highest with small farmers in all the seasons (6.00 to 9.00 litres). This variation in milk production could be attributed to the calving season of animals and type of fodder fed. The average per litre cost of production of buffalo milk in various seasons was observed to be lowest in marginal farms as compared to small farms (Rs. 1.17 to Rs. 1.59).

Sharma and Singh (1986) revealed that the overall total milk production per household in the dairy group has been computed to be 93.27 per cent higher than the non-dairy ones. Higher milk production in the dairy households could be attributed to the keeping of crossbred cows on the cattle holding.

Singh *et al.* (1986) conducted a survey in Operation Research Project of NDRI areas in the year 1983-84. The results revealed that the average gross cost for the maintenance of a local cow, buffalo and crossbred cow was about Rs. 2,344, Rs. 3,272 and Rs. 3,497 per annum; respectively. However, the average net income obtained from crossbred cow during the year was Rs. 890 as against only Rs. 56 from a buffalo and net loss of about Rs. 1,267 from a local cow. Interestingly, a crossbred cow generated average family labour income of about Rs. 1806 per annum as compared to Rs. 899 by a buffalo. However, local cow failed to provide positive family labour income. It was observed that the average net cost of milk production for local cows, buffaloes and crossbred cows was estimated at Rs. 4.01, Rs. 2.17 and Rs. 1.42 per litre, respectively.

The study undertaken by Sharma *et al.* (1986) during 1984-85 in rural and urban area of Gwalior district on factors affecting cost of milk production indicated that feed was the major component of expenditure on milk production, ranging between 43 per cent and 69 per cent, with an average of about 60 per cent of total expenditure. Feed cost was found to be lower in rural area (Rs. 547) and semi-urban area (Rs. 8.27), as compared to urban area (Rs. 10.30), as fodder based feeding was more in practice in rural and semi-urban area as compared to urban area. The cost of production was however lower in urban (Rs. 2.19) and semi-urban area (Rs. 2.11) as compared to rural area where it was Rs. 2.87. This was because of higher milk yield of 6.5 kg in urban and 7.00 kg in semi-urban area as compared to rural area, where it was 4.3 kgs. Labour cost was the second important cost component accounting for about 12 per cent to 24 per cent with an average of 19 per cent of total expenditure. Miscellaneous recurring expenses varied from 4.79 per cent to .79 per cent with an average of 5.63 per cent, whereas the fixed cost varied from 10 to 20 per cent with an average of about 15 per cent.

Patel, V.M. (1987) studied impact of milk co-operatives Gujarat, found that had created positive on the economy of milk producers and played a vital role for development of rural economy, ingot and that of the milk producers in particulars. The milk co-operative also gave assistance for various welfare programme/purposes and initiated many rural development activities in the village through various funds raised out of their savings.

Bawander, B. *et al.* (1987) while conducting study on the impact of dairy development programme observed that where high breed cows have been distributed without other dairy development infrastructure it has not substantially helped to improve the income among the poor. The formation of co-operative societies for the procurement and chilling of milk and provision for cattle fodder along with cattle distribution scheme have been identified as important steps necessary for improving the socio-economic status of rural poor.

Bal *et al.* (1987) concluded that dry fodder, concentrates, human labour and fodder accounted for 14.70, 16.76, 19.50 and 25.50 per cent of the total maintenance cost. The fixed cost, which included the allowances for interest and depreciation on milch animals, cattle shed and equipments, accounted for 20 per cent of the total maintenance cost.

Rekib *et al.* (1987) stated that feed, human labour, fixed cost and miscellaneous cost including medicines formed 60.63, 15.26, 22.48 and 1.63 per cent of the total expenditure, in that order, in buffalo milk production.

Kumar and Gupta (1988) noted that feed cost accounted for 61.43 per cent of the maintenance cost of buffalo and 61.51 per cent in the case of local cow and 73.43 per cent in crossbred cow; the feed cost worked out to 28.48 per cent, 30.02 per cent and 19.15 per cent, respectively. The per litre cost of milk production was lowest in crossbred cow due to its highest milk yield.

Vashist and Katiha (1988) observed that crossbred cows fared well in Himachal Pradesh in terms of high returns and feed conversion than desi cows, pure bred cows and buffaloes.

Gangwar *et al.* (1989) observed that the total maintenance cost increased with the increase in size of the farm and the operational cost accounted for 68 per cent of the of the total maintenance cost.

C. Madan Mohan's study (1989) study on 'Dairy Management in India (A Study in Andhra Pradesh) pointed out managerial deficiencies of Warangal district dairy i.e. over stabbing, the uneconomic strength of am power, low procurement, high overhead charges despite increase in milk sales. It further aims at democratisation of dairy industry by farming producers' co-operatives and consumer's councils so as to facilitate paying remunerative price to rural producer and supplying quality milk at reasonable price to consumer. The study basically examined the managerial aspects of dairying.

M. Verhagen (1990) in his paper operation Flood and the rural poor concluded that "Operation Flood can at best have only a quite limited impact in terms of income and employment generation among the poor. Especially the poorest, the land less labourers, constituting about the bottom 25 per cent of the rural population are by and large left out of the programme. The marginal farmers could benefit from the programme, but being generally small producers having few animals and of a low quality, their gains can only be small. In general, producers seemed to benefit more from the creation of stable out let for their milk and the supply of inputs than from increases in production . . . limited access to fodder, for landless and poor due to limited no access to fodder cultivation, not extending credit facility to the members by dairy co-operatives; are major barriers for promoting cross breading programme among poor. So operation Flood is less oriented towards rural poor than towards the better off."

Baviskar, B.S. (1990) in his study pointed out dairy co-operatives in Sanjaya and AMUL have brought many benefits to the milk producers in the village through providing a guaranteed market for milk at a fixed price, supply cattle feed at a reasonable cost, regular and efficient veterinary and extension services at the village and there is no parallel to what AMUL has done for the milk producers of kheda. So far reducing economic inequality is concerned he wrote "A charger proportion of the well-to-do than the small farmers are milk producers. The former have more buffaloes and derive greater benefits by supplying larger quantities of milk and since last 25 years they have not enlarged their herds due to the constants of space and family labour. On the other hand, the small farmers have clearly gained from the cooperatives, which help them earn additional income. But while dairying may add to the profits of the big farmers, it contributes to the survival and viability of the small ones. The marginal utility of the benefits derived from the co-operatives is much greater to the latter. In fact, about 90 per cent of the land less labourers is unable to take advantage of the co-operative. Thus, the effectiveness of dairy development programmes in reducing poverty is serially limited.

M. Savara (1990) studied "Dairy Development Amongst the Tribals in Surat District" found despite increasing quantity of milk produced by the small and marginal farmers and land less labourers, mostly tribals. In reality, it accrued very low income for them. In the word of author: "malnourishshments trap which is lowering the quality of livestock, and a high milky animal and calf mortality rate. In other words, the Surat dairy programme does not seem to be self-sustaining development programme. For its survival it requires the perpetual inflow of money in the form of subsidies so that new productive animals can be bought lack of alternative regular employment and income generating opportunity, and loan-cum-subsidy facility to purchase milch animal at half of the price and on loan eagerly accepted by tribals to start dairy enterprise despite the negligible return i.e. surpass income of Re. 0.47 per day with one milch animal for are location."

Mishra and Sharma (1990) using official estimates, discuss growth rates in milk production for two sub-periods, 1951-52 to 1971-72 and 1971-72 to 1987-88. The annual growth rate was one per cent in the first period and 5.5 per cent in the second. Their calculations based on feasible yield growth rates and growth rates of milk animals show that the rate was 2 per cent per year during the first period and only 3.5 per cent to 4 per cent during the second period. They argue that the difference between the two sets of estimates is due to the fact that official estimates user estimated production of milk for the first period and overestimated it for the second period by officials to defend operation Flood programme. Despite per capita availability of milk has indeed increased, the data furnished by authors indicate a falling trend in per capita milk consumption in rural areas and an increasing trend in urban areas a finding which has serious implications for policy Currently, India exports 3 and 4 million tonnes of liquid milk, largely to European Economic Community, reduced domestic availability of milk, and receives dairy commodity aid. They put it this trade is based on a strange logic of trying to achieve national self-reliance in milk production but at the same time transferring the means of achievement additional production elsewhere.

A study conducted in North Arcot district of Tamil Nadu by Thirunavu Kkarasu *et al.* (1991) found the impact of operation flood on the income and employment of the land less or the most vulnerable rural population has a strong empirical evidence that the programme is making a 'revolution' very quietly, but absolutely. The Scheduled tribe, Scheduled caste and other caste beneficiaries, out of total annual net income from all sources Rs. 4,766, Rs. 6,803 and Rs. 5,771 and livestock contributes Rs. 885 (18.56 per cent), Rs. 1,700 (25.00 per cent) and Rs. 2,197 (38.06 per cent) to net income of households respectively whereas non-dairy households of ST, SC and other castes net annual income depicted Rs. 3,896, Rs. 3,729 and Rs. 3,545 and livestock's contribution constitution nil Rs. 23 (0.60 per cent) Rs. 451 (26.21 per cent) respectively. The benefits of operation flood are mere skewed towards the upper castes than the lower castes. It is also intend out that to accelerate and sustain investment on rural infrastructure in the inaccessible areas as lack of adequate rural infrastructure may alienate the people from the development programme.

Rao *et al.* (1991) stated that in milk production of buffaloes, feed and fodder costs together accounted for 71 per cent of the total cost, of which concentrates constituted the major share; human labour accounted for about 9 per cent of the total cost.

J.M. Heredero's study (1992) on Milk Co-operatives and Tribal Poverty in Gujarat, concluded is as follows: the impact of the income from dairying can be better appreciated if we take into consideration the total income of the members. In Romgapura income from milk formed 33 per cent of the total income of a member between 1984 and 1986. In Nandagram, decentralised co-operative, income from milk, constituted 47 per cent of the total in 1984 and 55 per cent in 1985-86. The introduction of dairy farming has, thus, provided new income to tribal families to complement alternative sources of income. However, in 1984-85 only 51 per cent of the members of Rangapsrn and 63 per cent of the members of Nandagram supplied milk to the co-operative.

D.R. Shah's study (1992) on dairy co-operativization in Tribal areas in Gujarat with a view to examine comparative strength and weakness of Ananda Pattern modem dairy cooperative structure and traditional dairy co-operative structure, and socio-economic impact of the dairy co-operativzations on the life and culture of tribals. The study explained that the traditional dairy co-operative structure could not become an effective alternative for the co-operative dairying through the weaker tribal producers residing in the remote part of the district. The traditional cooperative structure suffers from the basic limitation arising out of local area specialisation, lack of integration and its exclusive dependence on nearby urban market. Ananda pattern dairy co-operative structure as it is well demonstrated by comparative analysis of the working modem Ananda pattern dairy co-operatives and traditional dairy co-operatives in the tribal area under study deserves the replication for development of dairying through rural poor producers. The comparative study of Choryasi co-operative (traditional type), has been compared with Ananda pattern co-operative namely, Sumul. The farmer shows that the greatest achievement is its survival due to provide higher price to producers owing to cheaper marketing and distribution arrangement, and retain its customers even by charging higher price by compensating them with better quality milk.

Sharma and Singh (1993) pointed out in their study in Himachal Pradesh, Hill Cattle Development Programme Operated districts of Kangra and Kullu, the farmers can increase their milk out put by feeding more concentrates to the animals and milk yield was higher it he winter season than in the summer and rainy seasons. By using regression coefficients, they concluded. That the optimisation of resources with the existing capital indicated the possibility of increasing the milk out put in crossbred cows and buffaloes by diverting a part of funds from green fodder, dry fodder and labour to concentrates. Readjustment of feed inputs can raise milk production in all seasons on both the dairy and non-dairy households

Atibudhi (1995) studied 80 households in Pipili block of Puri district in Orissa to find out the rationale for adopting dairy farming as a tool for income generation and employment creation. Results provided micro Level evidences in support of dairy enterprise as a measure for anti poverty programmes,

Dairy farming raised the income level of the beneficiaries by Rs. 2527, Rs. 2606 and Rs. 2210 for small and marginal farmers and landless, respectively. Additional productive employment was generated through dairying.

Gauraha (1995) examined and compared the cost structure and relative economics of milk production based on data collected from a sample of 18 urban and 24 rural dairy farms in Raipur district of Madhya Pradesh, The study brought out that average daily expenditure incurred on a much animal was higher in the urban area than in the rural area due to higher proportion of concentrate and green fodder fed to the animals. The average cost of production per litre of milk for crossbred cow came to Rs. 5.16 and 44 in urban and rural dairies respectively, while the corresponding figures for buffalo worked out to Rs. 6.32 and Rs. 6.33. The net returns were Rs. 3.84 and Rs. 4.68 per litre in the case of crossbred cow and buffalos milk respectively in the urban area. These were Rs. 2.55 and Rs. 3.67 in the rural area. The per day per animal yield of milk higher in crossbred cow than in buffaloes in both the areas. Koshta and Chandrakar (1995), from their survey found that a combination of bred and local buffaloes have produced more returns. Local cow breeds were economical in terms of milk production.

Manbhekar *et al.* (1995), reported that the cost of feed and fodder accounted for 60 per cent of the total cost and variable cost formed 84 per cent of cost of milk production.

Naik and Mohanty (1995) collected cost of milk production data from 50 households having cows in Khurda district of Orissa. This study revealed that number of dry cows was more varying from 41 to 44 per cent to the total. Feed including concentrates constituted major cost of milk production.

Rout and Tripathy (1995) studied milk marketing costs, margins, and price spread indifferent milk marketing channels in Khurda district and observed that (i) in the direct' selling of milk, the producers received 93 per cent of the price paid by the consumers. This did not cover the total cost of milk production. (ii) In the marketing channel having one middleman, producers could recover variable cost but not the cost of Production fully. (iii) In the marketing channel having three middleman the price received by the producer was to the extent of 50 per cent of the price paid by consumers.

Singh *et al.* (1995) studied the factors influencing milk production in Khurda block of Khurda district. In 1993-94, 61 households rearing cows and buffaloes were studied using Cobb-Douglas Production function. Results revealed (i) the superiority of buffaloes over cows in respect of 3 economic variables - feed cost, milk yield and milk prices, (ii) at the aggregate level concentrates fed to cows in milk yield more milk; and (iii) feeding of dry and green fodder did not have significant impact.

Singh, (1997) found that the feed milk relationship among purebred cattle and buffaloes maintained at the National Dairy Research Institute, Karnal. Cobb-Douglas production function was fitted by taking digestible crude protein (DCP), total digestible non-nitrogen (DNN), number of milking days, age and book value as the independent variables influencing the milk production. The coefficient of multiple determinations was 95 per cent in purebred zebu cows, 89 per cent in crossbred cows and 75 per cent in buffaloes. It was observed that DCP exerted a positive and significant impact on milk production in all the breeds. The marginal value productivity coefficient was the highest in Zebu cattle followed by buffaloes and crossbred cattle.

A close observation of the studies presented in this section reveals that there has been plethora of studies relating to dairying and rural development. However, studies relating to dairying and rural development in Orissa are seant in number. The present study has its relevance in investigating the issue in the context of Orissa.

Bhagyarathi Parida (2009) reported that OMFED launched low-fat skimmed milk and pineapple sip for the calorie-conscious on Saturday. The OMFED already sells 3.8 lakh litres of pure milk a day across the State.

The new skimmed milk contains 0.5 per cent fat and about 8.7 per cent protein. The milk costs at Rs 8.50 for half litre pack and Rs 17 for one litre pack. It will be available in Bhubaneswar, Cuttack and adjacent towns from September 20 and later marketed in other areas of the state, said OMFED Chairman Suresh Mohapatra said. He, however, said there will be no hike in milk prices in the coming days. "Despite increasing the procurement price by Rs 2, we could manage to sell milk at the old prices and tried not to put extra burden on our customers," he said.

The state-run milk federation also has some expansion plans. It has been decided to set up eight automatic packing machines, which can augment production by three to four times.

Under the plan, OMFED with about 5000 retail outlets and 12 production centres is going to set up a 3000 litre per day capacity ice-cream plant at an investment of nearly Rs two crore. The ice cream plant is expected to start production by May 2010. In 2008-09, OMFED had an annual turnover of Rs 270 crore, which the officials claimed to be about Rs 310 crore, this year with a growth rate of 20 per cent.

# 3

# Dairy Development in Orissa

Next to agriculture, livestock occupies a prominent place in the rural economy of Orissa. According to Government of India reports, the total livestock population of Orissa in 2001 was 6.02 lakhs as against 2.17 lakhs in the year 1961. Since time immemorial, the importance of bovine stock has been realised by our ancestors even before using them in agriculture. There has been long standing custom based on belief and faith that gift of cow enhances virtue. People give cow during religious ceremonies and for the sake of emancipation of a departed person in maturity rites and to the daughter as dowry during her marriage. The cow provides food (milk), its dung used to clean the mud house and in agricultural land as fertiliser.

During those days milk was plenty as big herds of cows were maintained by the people. Every village had its own pasture lands and forest areas around it for common grazing. Bovine stock was an indication of wealth and prosperity of the family (Samal 1988).

## EVOLUTION OF LIVESTOCK POLICY IN ORISSA

During British rule no step had been taken to improve the condition of farmers and farm animals. It was in 1926; the British government appointed a Royal Commission on

Agriculture to study the conditions of agriculture and livestock and recommended the government for improvement of them. According to its recommendations, the Imperial Council of Agricultural Research (presently, Indian Council of Agricultural Research) was established in 1930 to coordinate research into various problems relating to agriculture and animal husbandry (GOI 1976).

The formation of Orissa Cattle Breeding Association "The Utkal Gomangal Samitee" in 1936 constitutes the turning point for the development of dairy in Orissa. At the same time, the then Viceroy Lord Linlithgow realised that he development of farmers rest in development of livestock. So provincial governments were advised to develop dual-purpose cattle for providing milk and for draft labour in agriculture. For upgrading the livestock situation in the provincial State, Haryana and Red Sindhi bulls were purchased during 1937 for breeding of goat and improved cows (Samal, 1988).

Till date, Utkal Gomangal Samittee (UGS) has been working very closely with Fisheries and Animal Resource Development Department. The UGS support the ARD in several aspects of livestock development. The activities of UGS include:

(1) establishment of bull centres for natural breeding,

(2) supply of liquid nitrogen for artificial insemination,

(3) heifer rearing farms,

(4) supply of milch animals (about 350 per annum),

(5) supply of concentrate food,

(6) establishment of cattle feed plants,

(7) fodder programme,

(8) enrichment of paddy straw,

(9) cattle infertility and disease treatment camps,

(10) education and training of farmers and

(11) Animal husbandry pilot programme about selected urban growth centres.

After merger of Bolangir and Sundergarh feudatory States in 1948 in Orissa, Red Sindhi bulls which were available there were sent to Gop area of Puri and Haryana bulls to villages in Cuttack district. Artificial insemination (AI) was first started in 1949 by Dr. Debeswar Konhar, who had been trained in the subject at the IVRI, Izatnagar (Samal, 1988). Having proved fruitful by increasing milk yield of cattle in the area, it was the first step in the State to develop productivity of livestock by adoption of modem technology.

After independence, the Government of Orissa being realised the deficiency of milch animals tried to improve the buffalo bull for breeding of indigenous buffaloes of any State these buffaloes are called, *murrah* in Punjab because their horns were curved). The upgraded pregnancies were bigger in size and yielded more milk. Utkal Gomangal Samitte purchased a large number of such bulls and maintained as study in buffalo populated areas. Again in 1949-50, selective breeding of best types of indigenous cattle of Orissa namely, Binjharpur, Glumsari and Khariari cattle were taken up but discontinued soon after realising satisfactory results required long years to achieve.

In 1964, Government of India instructed State Governments not to encourage buffalo breeding in government firms as in big cities the buffaloes were replaced by milk cattle under the apprehension that cows might be affected by it which were revered by Hindus. But this was not a case for Orissa. So it was continued to breed buffaloes as for dairy purposes by our veterinary officers (Samal, 1988).

During planned development era, in Orissa steps had been taken to improve livestock wealth, because around which the most of rural economic activities evolves. The government started key village schemes for development of our bovine stock to undertake artificial insemination and combat contagious diseases from 1952. At present, there are 238 key village units operating in 23 key village blocks and there are four intensive cattle development projects (IDCP) divided into 16 ICD zones and 330 ICD units operating in Orissa. In 1958, the National Rinderpeste Eradication scheme came into operation in Orissa to control the rinder pest disease of the bovine stock. In 1964, cross breeding with exotic bulls for milk production in urban areas of Orissa started and subsequently reached in adjacent rural areas. In 1978, use of frozen semen technology started from big pedigreed bulls for Artificial Insemination (AI) through Danish assistance. It has become popular and in 1993 out of 2021 livestock centres, it was 1430 frozen semen AI centres serving in Orissa of which 252 centres are pure AI centres. There have two frozen semen banks with bull stations are functioning at Cuttack and Bhawanipatna. The Utkal Gomangal Samiti is maintaining quality buffalo bulls at 277 centres in remote rural areas for natural services and AI. The latest technology for development of quality of our bovine stock, and bull is knowns "Embryo Transfer (ET) is being adopted in the state with the help of OMFED".

## BOVINE STOCK IN ORISSA

In any rural economy like Orissa the purpose of maintaining livestock is enormous and manifold. The contribution of bovine stock is mainly realised in the form of (i) food (milk and milk products), (ii) Energy (draught and traction power for agriculture, rural transport, industries i.e. *Khandesaries, gur* oil extraction, grinding animal dung as crop manure and fuel for cooking and heating by means of dung cake, bio-gas and (iii) raw materials (in the form of wool, hairs, hides, hoof, bones skins and horns of fallen or slaughtered animal.

From the point of view of dairying cow and the buffaloes are only maintained in Orissa for milking purpose whereas goats and sheep for meat only. The trend of livestock population Orissa is presented in Table 3.1.

As per 2001 livestock causes cattle population and buffalo population are 138.10 lakhs and 9.01 lakhs respectively. The total bovine population thus stands at 151.98 lakhs as against the total bovine population of 150.86 lakhs in 1991 out of Orissa's total cattle population only 5.63 lakhs (4.15%) are crossbred cattle as per 1991 census, in 1982, census there were 190.30 lakhs of cattle, 13.33 lakhs of buffaloes constituting our bovine stock (142.62 lakhs). The percentage increase of bovine stock in Orissa in 1991 over 91982 is 5.8 per cent of which 5.0 per cent increase are found for cattle and 13.2 per cent increase for buffaloes. This indicates the proportionate increase in buffalo population is marginally on the higher side. The crossbred cattle which were 2.26 lakhs in 1982 increased to 5.63 lakhs during 1991 registering an increase to the extent of 148.76 per cent. Similarly in percentage terms, crossbred cattle constituting 1.75 per cent of the cattle population in 1982, encounter 4.15 per cent of the cattle population in 1995. in 1995, there were 7.44 lakh crossbred cows which increased to 8.70 lakhs. Thus in comparison to 1981, in 2001 over 20 years time period, there has been 286.72 per cent increase in cattle population).

It is found from Table 3.1, that the marginal increase in buffalo population shows a rising trend up to the year 1972. Thereafter, the proportion of buffaloes to total bovine population slightly declines.

## DISTRICT-WISE COVERAGE OF CATTLE AND BUFFALO POPULATION

Orissa has a large livestock population of over 23 million head as per the latest livestock census (Table 3.1) cattle constitute the primary livestock asset for nearly 60 per cent of the total livestock population followed by goats.

Orissa comprises three main urban centres namely Bhubaneswar, Cuttack and Puri. These places serve as the main marketing centres. Due to proximity to these urban centres and overall better infrastructure livestock population denoting in higher in northern coastal districts of Balasore, Jeypore, Bhadrak, Cuttack, Puri and Jagatsinghpur. These districts account for a quarter of the livestock population of the state, although geographically they cover only about 12% of the area on the other hand, the southern and interior districts of Rayagada, Phulbani, Koraput, Kalahandi, Malkangiri, Sundergarh and Mayurbhanj which occupy appropriately 40 per cent of the geographical area of the State accounting for 30 per cent of the livestock population (Table 3.2).

**Table 3.1 : Livestock Population in Orissa (in '000 Nos.)**

| Sl. No. | Year Bovine | Cattle | Buffalo | Total | Sheep | Goat | Others |
|---|---|---|---|---|---|---|---|
| 0 | 1 | 2 | 3 | 4 | 5 | 6 | 7 |
| 1 | 1956 | 8220 (90.2) | 888 (9.8) | 9108 (100.0) | 1117 | 1695 | 129 |
| 2 | 1961 | 9810 (90.1) | 1075 (9.9) | 10885 (100.0) | 994 | 2382 | 217 |
| 3 | 1966 | 10628 (89.3) | 1269 (10.7) | 118.97 (100.0) | 1182 | 3082 | 180 |
| 4 | 1972 | 11496 (89.1) | 1399 (10.9) | 12895 (100.0) | 1369 | 2884 | 387 |
| 5 | 1977 | 12121 (90.0) | 1350 (10.0) | 13471 (100.0) | 1432 | 3416 | 295 |
| 6 | 1982 | 12930 (90.7) | 1333 (9.3) | 14263 (100.0) | 1990 | 4931 | 418 |
| 7 | 1991 | 13577 (90.0) | 1509 (10.0) | 15086 (100.0) | 1841 | 4804 | 540 |
| 8 | 1995 | 14766 (89.9) | 1652 (10.1) | 16418 (100.0) | 1865 | 5412 | 572 |
| 9 | 2001 | 13810 (90.9) | 1388 (9.01) | 15198 (100.0) | 1779 | 5880 | 602 |

**Table 3.2 : District-wise Cattle and Buffalo Population in Orissa (in '000)**

| Sl. No. | District | Cattle | Buffalo | Total |
|---|---|---|---|---|
| 1. | Angul | 521.4 | 512.6 | 1034 |
| 2. | Balasore | 912.8 | 7.1 | 919.9 |
| 3. | Bargarh | 513.1 | 39.1 | 552.2 |
| 4. | Bhadrak | 550.1 | 14.2 | 564.3 |
| 5. | Bolangir | 599.0 | 117.0 | 716 |
| 6. | Boudh | 231.8 | 35.6 | 267.4 |
| 7. | Cuttack | 640.9 | 62.5 | 703.4 |
| 8. | Deogarh | 181.3 | 21.0 | 202.3 |
| 9. | Dhenkanal | 487.2 | 75.0 | 562.2 |
| 10. | Gajapati | 272.7 | 18.1 | 290.8 |
| 11. | Ganjam | 1029.3 | 151.8 | 1181.1 |
| 12. | Jagatsinghpur | 437.8 | 15.8 | 453.6 |
| 13. | Jajpur | 634.0 | 11.9 | 645.9 |
| 14. | Jharsuguda | 193.3 | 21.2 | 214.5 |
| 15. | Kalahandi | 540.2 | 125.9 | 666.1 |
| 16. | Kendrapada | 308.7 | 76.2 | 384.9 |
| 17. | Keonjhar | 471.1 | 22.1 | 493.2 |
| 18. | Khurda | 695.9 | 37.8 | 733.7 |
| 19. | Koraput | 424.7 | 143.2 | 567.9 |
| 20. | Malkangiri | 366.7 | 39.0 | 405.7 |
| 21. | Mayurbhanj | 894.5 | 31.2 | 925.7 |
| 22. | Nuapada | 380.3 | 106.9 | 487.2 |
| 23. | Nayagarh | 390.6 | 62.3 | 452.9 |
| 24. | Nabarangpur | 289.6 | 70.2 | 359.8 |
| 25. | Phulbani | 461.3 | 26.2 | 487.5 |
| 26. | Puri | 405.4 | 115.3 | 520.7 |
| 27. | Rayagada | 566.9 | 25.4 | 592.3 |
| 28. | Sambalpur | 429.4 | 36.5 | 465.9 |
| 29. | Sonepore | 258.3 | 30.0 | 288.3 |
| 30. | Sundergarh | 676.1 | 60.9 | 737 |
| | Total | 14765.9 | 1652.0 | 16417.9 |

**Source**: Directorate of Animal Husbandry and Veterinary Services, Cuttack , 2004

A large proportion of the cattle are buffalo population in Orissa are of non-descript, indigenous type. Overall the proportion of crossbred is less than five per cent. Furthermore, a significant proportion of the crossbred population is concentrated around the towns of Bhubaneswar, Puri and Cuttack.

## TRENDS OF MILK PRODUCTION IN ORISSA

Total milk production in Orissa has grown over time at roughly the same rate as per India as a whole (Table 3.3).

**Table 3.3 : Trends of Milk Production and Per Capita Availability of Milk in Orissa**

| Sl. No. | Milk Year (000'mt) | Per Capita Production of Milk Per Day | Availability |
|---|---|---|---|
| 0 | 1 | 2 | 3 |
| 1. | 1972-73 | 196.00 | N.A. |
| 2. | 1973-74 | 200.00 | N.A. |
| 3. | 1974-80 | 238.00 | N.A. |
| 4. | 1980-81 | 310.00 | N.A. |
| 5. | 1981-82 | 316.01 | 27 |
| 6. | 1982-83 | 322.44 | 33 |
| 7. | 1983-84 | 344.49 | 34 |
| 8. | 1984-85 | 386.10 | 37 |
| 9. | 1985-86 | 394.29 | 32 |
| 10. | 1986-87 | 400.79 | 38 |
| 11. | 1987-88 | 423.16 | 39 |
| 12. | 1988-89 | 434.04 | 39 |
| 13. | 1989-90 | 454.55 | 40 |
| 14. | 1990-91 | 471.00 | 38 |
| 15. | 1991-92 | 505.00 | 41 |
| 16. | 1992-93 | 542.00 | 43 |

*(contd.)*

| 0 | 1 | 2 | 3 |
|---|---|---|---|
| 17. | 1993-94 | 560.00 | 47 |
| 18. | 1994-95 | 590.00 | 48 |
| 19. | 1995-96 | 625.00 | 50 |
| 20. | 1996-97 | 669.92 | 52 |
| 21. | 1997-98 | 671.83 | 64 |
| 22. | 1998-99 | 733.00 | 65 |
| 23. | 1999-00 | 847.78 | 67 |
| 24. | 2000-01 | 875.00 | 70 |
| 25. | 2001-02 | 929.00 | 70 |
| 26. | 2002-03 | 941.00 | 71 |
| 27. | 2003-04 | 995.08 | 74 |
| 28. | 2004-05(P) | 1282.76 | 92 |

**Source:** Compiled from different issues of *Economics Survey*, Government of Orissa.

The analysis of time series data (from 1972-73 to 2004-05) on milk production and per capita milk availability per day indicates that there has been a continuous increase in the trend of milk production in Orissa over the years ($R^2$ = 0.9011). However, the rate increase slowed down upto the year 1999-2000. But, since 1999-2000 the production of milk in Orissa is rising at an increasing rate. The per capita availability of milk in Orissa also fluctuates between 27 gram. in 1980-81 to 52 g in 1996-97. In the year 2000-01, it was 70 g and 92 g in the year 2004-05. However over the years, an increasing trend is noticed on the per capita availability of milk per day ($R^2$ = 0.9027).

Crossbred cows contribute more than 35 per cent of the total milk production in Orissa although they only constitute about 6 per cent of the total bovine population. Furthermore, the contribution of crossbred cows to total milk production has steadily increased from about 10 per cent in 1981-82 to nearly 37 per cent in 1996-97.

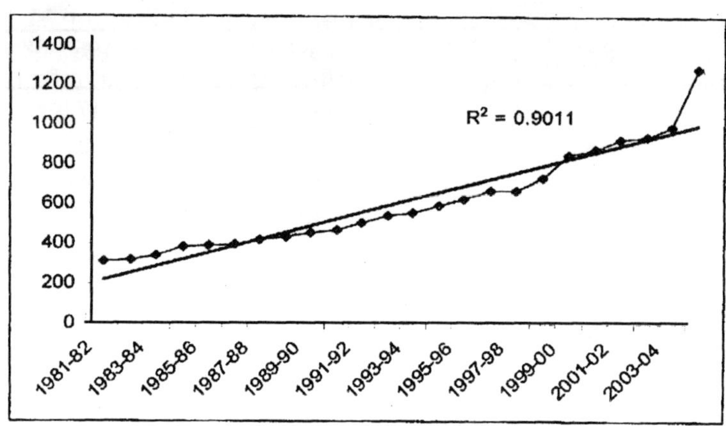


**Fig. 3.1: Trends in Milk Production (1981-2004)**

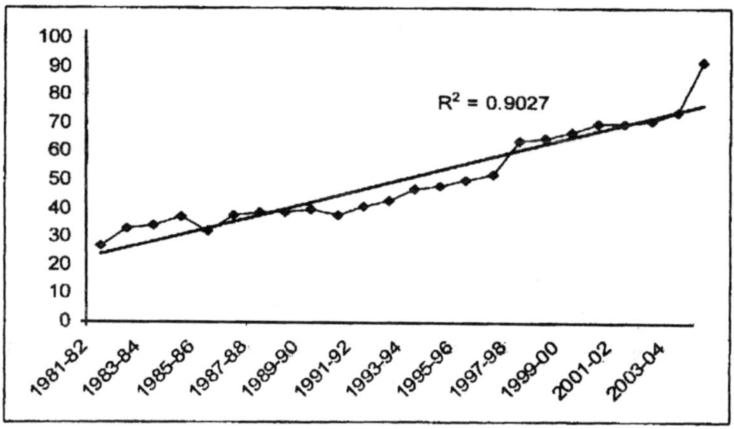


**Fig. 3.2: Trends in per capita per day availability of milk in Orissa (1981-2004)**

## MILK YIELD PER MILCH ANIMALS

It is revealed from Table 3.4 that up to the year 1987-88, milk yield per milch animal per day was estimated considering only nondescript cows. However, in the year 1991-92, milk yield was separately estimated for non-descript and crossbred cows. This system continues till now. In case of crossbred cows per capita per day yield of milk was 0.51 kg in 19085-86 which is found decreased to 0.445 in 1987-88 in 1991 onwards it is found that PCPDYM for non-descript cows continuously declines over years. On the other hand, PCPDYM for crossbred cows watershed 4 times higher than the non-descript cows and it was 6 times higher in 2001-02 similarly, PCPDYM for buffaloes tends to increase over time.

**Table 3.4 : Milk Yield per Milch Animals in Orissa (per day in kg)**

| Particulars | 1985-86 | 1986-87 | 1987-88 | 1990-91 | 1991-92 | 2000-01 | 2000-02 |
|---|---|---|---|---|---|---|---|
| Non-descript | 0.513 | 0.512 | 0.445 | 0.443 | 0.442 | | 0.48 |
| Cow | | | 2.597 | 2.984 | | | 3.93 |
| Buffaloe | 1.214 | 1.292 | 1.334 | 1.448 | 1.458 | 1.485 | 1.84 |
| Crossbred | | | | | | | |

**Source:** Compiled from different issues of *Economics Survey*, Government of Orissa.

## COMPARATIVE PERFORMANCE OF ORISSA IN MILK YIELD PER MILCH ANIMAL

The comparative performance of different milch animals with respect to milk yield in Orissa in relation to other States is presented in Table 3.5. It is found that the performance of Orissa with respect to milk yield among all categories of milk animals is abysmally lower because in all the states shown in Table 3.5, the milk production in Orissa is the lowest.

## PER CAPITA PER DAY MILK AVAILABILITY IN ORISSA

Time-series data on per capita per day milk availability in Orissa as against India is presented Table 3.6. It is revealed that though there has been a continuous increase in per capita per day milk availability in Orissa as well as India, the gap between Orissa and India tends to widen over years. However, the gap has been declining from 2002-03 till date. Even though Orissa is implementing Operation Flood Programme, it has failed to achieve the desired results on the ground of continuous increase in the gap between per capita per day availability milk in Orissa and India.

**Table 3.5 : Orissa's Performance in Milk Yield per milch animal in relation to other States**

| Sl. | States | Indigenous | Crossbred | |
|---|---|---|---|---|
| No. | | Cow | Cow | Buffalo |
| 1. | Andhra Pradesh | 1.34 | 5.07 | 2.89 |
| 2. | Bihar | 1.63 | 4.81 | 3.50 |
| 3. | Gujarat | 2.84 | 7.96 | 3.80 |
| 4. | Haryana | 4.11 | 6.52 | 5.64 |
| 5. | Himachal Pradesh | 1.69 | 3.32 | 3.02 |
| 6. | Karnataka | 1.82 | 5.57 | 2.40 |
| 7. | Kerala | 2.22 | 5.63 | 4.83 |
| 8. | Madhya Pradesh | 1.18 | 5.56 | 2.98 |
| 9. | Maharashtra | 1.50 | 6.79 | 3.56 |
| 10. | Orissa | 0.48 | 3.93 | 1.84 |
| 11. | Punjab | 2.88 | 8.36 | 5.62 |
| 12. | Rajasthan | 2.79 | 5.31 | 4.01 |
| 13. | Tamil Nadu | 2.39 | 5.55 | 3.58 |
| 14. | Uttar Pradesh | 2.04 | 5.80 | 3.74 |
| 15. | West Bengal | 2.15 | 7.82 | 6.26 |
| 16. | All India | 1.86 | 6.16 | 3.94 |

**Source:** GOI, Basic Animal Husbandry statistics, Department of Animal Husbandry and Dairying, Ministry of Agriculture, Government of India.

## INSTITUTIONAL STRUCTURE AND INFRASTRUCTURE FOR SERVICE DELIVERY

Animal husbandry is a state subject in India. Livestock Assistance Centre (LACs) operated by the Directorate of

Animal Husbandry and Veterinary Services (DAHVs) under the Fisheries and Animal Resources Development Department of the Government of Orissa are the primary source of veterinary services in the latest. These centres provide curative health, artificial insemination and various extension services. In 1996, there were about 3500 centres about 550 veterinary hospitals and dispensaries and 3000 livestock aid centres in the state. The District wise coverage of veterinary institutions is shows in Table 3.7.

**Table 3.6 : Per Capita per Day Milk in Availability in Orissa and in India (in grams)**

| Sl. No. | Year | India | Orissa | Gap |
|---|---|---|---|---|
| 1. | 1950-51 | 132 | 29 | 103 |
| 2. | 1955-56 | 135 | 27 | 108 |
| 3. | 1960-61 | 127 | 26 | 101 |
| 4. | 1965-66 | 108 | 25 | 83 |
| 5. | 1969-70 | 107 | 24 | 83 |
| 6. | 1970-71 | 105 | 23 | 82 |
| 7. | 1977-78 | 112 | 23 | 89 |
| 8. | 1981-82 | 123 | 27 | 96 |
| 9. | 1985-86 | 136 | 32 | 104 |
| 10. | 1990-91 | 162 | 38 | 124 |
| 11. | 1991-92 | 176 | 41 | 135 |
| 12. | 1992-93 | 178 | 43 | 135 |
| 13. | 1999-00 | 180 | 67 | 113 |
| 14. | 2000-01 | 192 | 70 | 122 |
| 15. | 2001-02 | 226 | 70 | 156 |
| 16. | 2002-03 | 228 | 67 | 161 |
| 17. | 2003-04 | 231 | 74 | 157 |
| 18. | 2004-05 | 232 | 92 | 140 |

**Source:** Ministry of Agriculture, Government of India and Department of Animal Husbandry, Government of Orissa.

**Table 3.7 : District-wise Coverage of Veterinary Institutions in Orissa**

| District | No. of Veterinary Hospitals and Dispensaries | No. of Livestock Aid Centres | Total | Geographical Area per sq. km | No. of Anim. Large Rumi. |
|---|---|---|---|---|---|
| 0 | 1 | 2 | 3 | 4 | 5 |
| Balasore | 21 | 114 | 135 | 29.63 | 7065.19 |
| Bhadrak | 13 | 99 | 112 | 26.79 | 5110.71 |
| Bolangir | 21 | 114 | 135 | 51.85 | 4506.67 |
| Sonepur | 10 | 37 | 47 | 42.55 | 5748.94 |
| Cuttack | 25 | 151 | 176 | 22.73 | 3752.27 |
| Jeypore | 19 | 119 | 138 | 21.74 | 4672.46 |
| Jagatsinghpur | 13 | 109 | 122 | 16.39 | 2465.57 |
| Kendrapada | 14 | 47 | 61 | 49.18 | 4180.33 |
| Dhenkanal | 18 | 86 | 104 | 48.08 | 5379.81 |
| Angul | 16 | 78 | 94 | 63.83 | 6464.89 |
| Ganjam | 37 | 236 | 274 | 29.30 | 3563.74 |
| Gajapati | 11 | 49 | 60 | 50.00 | 4413.33 |
| Kalahandi | 21 | 122 | 143 | 55.94 | 4032.17 |
| Nuapada | 8 | 62 | 70 | 47.14 | 3442.86 |
| Keonjhar | 22 | 118 | 140 | 57.14 | 5355.71 |
| Koraput | 25 | 112 | 137 | 65.69 | 4369.34 |
| Malkangiri | 13 | 51 | 64 | 93.75 | 6856.25 |
| Nawarangpur | 17 | 66 | 83 | 60.24 | 5571.08 |
| Rayagada | 16 | 85 | 101 | 79.21 | 4693.07 |
| Mayurbhanj | 42 | 161 | 203 | 54.19 | 4456.16 |
| Phulbani | 20 | 112 | 132 | 45.45 | 2783.33 |
| Boudh | 7 | 25 | 32 | 125.00 | 8625.00 |
| Purl | 15 | 145 | 160 | 18.75 | 2991.88 |
| Khurda | 20 | 166 | 186 | 16.13 | 2290.86 |
| Nayagarh | 16 | 68 | 84 | 47.62 | 4425.00 |

*(contd.)*

| 0 | 1 | 2 | 3 | 4 | 5 |
|---|---|---|---|---|---|
| Sambalpur | 18 | 107 | 125 | 56.00 | 3472.00 |
| Bargarh | 19 | 126 | 145 | 41.38 | 3757.93 |
| Deogarh | 4 | 20 | 24 | 125.00 | 7995.83 |
| Jharsuguda | 9 | 36 | 45 | 44.44 | 4106.67 |
| Sundergarh | 30 | 116 | 146 | 68.49 | 5311.64 |
| Total | 540 | 2937 | 44.95 | 4362.24 | 3.477 |

**Source:** Ministry of Agriculture Government of India and Department of Animal Husband

## INSTITUTIONAL EFFORTS FOR DAIRY DEVELOPMENT IN ORISSA

The working group appointed by the Government of India in 1962 stressed the need to develop dairying and animal husbandry throughout cooperative effort. Accordingly the National Dairy Development Board (NDDB) at Anand (Gujarat) was constituted in 1965 by Dr. Verghese Kurein. It was in 1970 that NDDB launched Operation Flood with the objective of putting India on the top of the world map in milk production. Accordingly Government of India setup the Indian Dairy Corporation (IDC) in 1970 at Boroda to execute the Operation Flood Programme.

Though operation flood in its 1st phase was commenced from July 1970, but, Orissa could not avail the benefit of operation flood. This phase of operation flood continued from 1970-75 in the States of Andhra Pradesh, Bihar, Gujarat, Haryana, Maharashtra, Punjab, Rajasthan, Tamil Nadu , Uttar Pradesh, West Bengal and Delhi.

However, the Operation Flood II programme which was launched under the aegis of National Dairy development Board was implemented in Orissa from 1982, covering four erstwhile undivided districts viz. Cuttack, Dhenkanal, Keonjhar and Puri. With the implementation of Operation Flood II programme, the Orissa State Cooperative Milk Producers' Federation

(OMFED) was registered in 1980-81 and became operational from October 1980. The OMFED followed Anand Pattern of dairy cooperative principle with the financial assistance of Indian Dairy Corporation, technical know-how of National Dairy Development Board and due patronage of the State Government, the OMFED implemented the intensive dairy development programme in Orissa.

The third phase of the Operation Flood (1985-1994) enabled dairy cooperatives to rapidly build up the basic infrastructure required to produce and market more and more milk daily. The Operation Flood III programmes were started in all the districts in 1987 except Sambalpur which was included from August 1989.

The Operation Flood programmes function in a free manner in the State. At the grass-root level, there are village level cooperative societies called the 'primary milk producers cooperative societies' and these primary societies are federated into district milk producers union at the district level. The District Milk Producers Union is affiliated to the Orissa Milk Federation, known as the State Milk Producers' Federation. This State level federation is the apex and legal organisation.

## THE ORISSA MILK PRODUCERS FEDERATION

The OMFED is a three tire mechanism, of which at the village level there are primary milk producers cooperative society, at the district level, there are District Milk Unions and OMFED is the State level federation. At the beginning stage of OMFED only four districts as Puri, Cuttack, Dhenkanal and Keonjhar constituted the operational area. In the second phase, some more districts such as Sambalpur, Ganjam, Sundergarh, Balasore and Kalahandi were included under the operational area of OMFED. So far, 371 milk producers' cooperative societies have been formed consisting of 15,949 members.

The activity of OMFED is conducted by a Board of Directors which as a Chainnan to the affiliated milk union, three nominees on behalf of the Government of Orissa, one nominee from NDDB and Managing Director of the Federation (who is an ex-officio member).

The Chainnan is an elected person by the members. The number of functional dairy cooperative societies in Orissa is presented in Table 3.8. Since the introduction of operation flood programme in Orissa during early 1980s, there has been continuous expansion in the number of dairy cooperatives in Orissa. In the year 1980-81, there were 52 functional dairy cooperatives with 3328 members. By 2003, there were 1015 dairy cooperatives with 1,15,000 members. During this period, there has been around 19 times increase in the number of functional cooperatives and 34 times increase in membership.

**Table 3.8 : Functional Dairy Cooperative Societies in Orissa**

| Sl. No. | Year | No. of Societies | Member-ship | Per Society Member-ship | Additional Member During the year |
|---|---|---|---|---|---|
| 1. | 1980-81 | 52 | 3328 | 64.00 | - |
| 2. | 1981-82 | 95 | 4763 | 50.13 | 1435 |
| 3. | 1982-83 | 151 | 7950 | 52.64 | 3187 |
| 4. | 1984-85 | 209 | 12527 | 59.93 | 2378 |
| 5. | 1985-86 | 270 | 15949 | 59.07 | 3422 |
| 6. | 1986-87 | 273 | 17590 | 64.43 | 1641 |
| 7. | 1987-88 | 390 | 24217 | 62.09 | 6627 |
| 8. | 1989-90 | 549 | 40804 | 74.32 | 8633 |
| 9. | 1990-91 | 610 | 46467 | 79.68 | 5363 |
| 10. | 1991-92 | 663 | 51903 | 78.28 | 5436 |
| 11. | 1992-93 | 762 | 54547 | 77.70 | 2644 |
| 12. | 1993-94 | 775 | 60685 | 78.30 | 6138 |
| 13. | 1994-95 | 814 | 66744 | 81.99 | 6059 |
| 14. | 1998-99 | 1055 | - | - | - |
| 15. | 2002-03 | 1015 | 115000 | 133.30 | - |

**Source:** Compiled from different issues of *Economic Survey*, Govt. of Orissa.

Bhagyarathi Parida (2009) reported that OMFED launched low-fat skimmed milk and pineapple sip for the calorie-conscious on Saturday. The OMFED already sells 3.8 lakh litres of pure milk a day across the State. The new skimmed milk contains 0.5 per cent fat and about 8.7 per cent protein. The milk costs at Rs 8.50 for half litre pack and Rs 17 for one litre pack. It will be available in Bhubaneswar, Cuttack and adjacent towns from September 20 and later marketed in other areas of the state, said OMFED Chairman Suresh Mohapatra said. He, however, said there will be no hike in milk prices in the coming days. "Despite increasing the procurement price by Rs 2, we could manage to sell milk at the old prices and tried not to put extra burden on our customers," he said. The state-run milk federation also has some expansion plans. It has been decided to set up eight automatic packing machines, which can augment production by three to four times. Under the plan, OMFED with about 5000 retail outlets and 12 production centres is going to set up a 3000 litre per day capacity ice-cream plant at an investment of nearly Rs two crore. The ice cream plant is expected to start production by May 2010. In 2008-09, OMFED had an annual turnover of Rs 270 crore, which the officials claimed to be about Rs 310 crore, this year with a growth rate of 20 per cent.

## INSTITUTIONAL DEVELOPMENT FOR DAIRY DEVELOPMENT

The Working Group appointed by the Government of India in 1962 stressed the need to develop dairying and animal husbandry through cooperative effort. Accordingly the National Dairy Development (NDDB) at Anand (Gujarat) constituted in 1965; as a programme launching body, was not authorised to transact any financial and commercial activities, the Union Government set up the Indian Dairy Corporation (IDC) in 1970 at Baroda to execute the (Operation Flood) programme which is first of its kind in Third World countries, with a financial grant of Rs. 95 crores (Government of India Forth Five-year Plan). It was primarily decided by the Council of European Economic Community (EEC) Ministers meeting held on April 1969, to include for the first time dairy products with in its food aid programme and consequently allocated during

**Table 3.9: Sale of Milk and Milk Products by OMFED from 2000-01 to 2008-09**

| | 2000-01 | 2001-02 | 2002-03 | 2003-04 | 2004-05 | 2005-06 | 2006-07 | 2007-08 | 2008-09 |
|---|---|---|---|---|---|---|---|---|---|
| Milk sale (LPD) | 103832 | 105934 | 114176 | 148392 | 174219 | 318213 | 354368 | 361439 | 363580 |
| Ghee sale (mt) | 443.396 | 435.547 | 387.758 | 302.918 | 327.968 | 413.704 | 367.388 | 395.334 | 389.61 |
| S.F.M. sale (Bottle) | 581194 | 1073168 | 1627372 | 1326667 | 1418433 | 161766 | 1476438 | 1579778 | 1635986 |
| Sweet Curd Sale (M.T) | 307.176 | 323.122 | 372.252 | 283.912 | 334.04 | 547.296 | 596.839 | 752.29 | 739.105 |
| Butter sale (M.T) | 5.77 | 5.155 | 3.442 | 6.831 | 86.15 | 10.03 | 6.879 | 11.147 | 12.16 |
| Plain Curd sale (M.T) | 80.309 | 145.993 | 319.647 | 596.388 | 1388.6 | 2265.85 | 2374.183 | 2870.886 | 3802.126 |
| Butter Milk (Pkts/Nos.) | 1055168 | 1330487 | 2043340 | 1755908 | 1947390 | 4176558 | 3364684 | 4545185 | 5947118 |
| Paneer (M.T) | 0 | 0 | 124.246 | 193.565 | 293.927 | 352.045 | 231.392 | 332.042 | 545.811 |
| Chennapoda (M.T) | 0 | 0 | 38.182 | 46.081 | 40.649 | 33.23 | 16.399 | 17.071 | 38.732 |
| Lassi (Nos/Pkts) | 0 | 0 | 214510 | 549788 | 713214 | 1382556 | 1503606 | 1886983 | 2478910 |

**Source:** *Annual Report 2009*, OMFED

that year 35,000 tonnes of butter oil (130) and 123,000 tonnes of skimmed milk powder to the World Food Programme, which channelled most of it to India's operation flood programme (Van Dorsten, 1986). The aim of OF-I was inaugurated on October 2, 1978 with a greater allocation of Rs. 485 crores (NDDII: 1979). Batra *et al.* (1979) pointed out that the OF-II is aimed at raising the nutritional standards of the people, generating employment and augmenting the income in rural areas through a viable subsidiary occupation. The 01: may be considered a socioeconomic model for dairy development characterised by three features, i.e. (a) creation of a specific type of milk cooperative at village level in the light of Anand model; (b) creation of union level milk processing plants owned by the cooperatives which form a market out let for their liquid milk at fair prices; (c) creation of metropolitan dairies providing city dwellers with hygienic liquid from the unions which the cooperate at state level in federations (doorknobs, *et al.* 1987). The OF-I was inoperative in Orissa whereas OF-II started realizing its functioning after the Orissa state Cooperative Milk Producers Federation Ltd. (OMFED) comes into being in 1980-81. it was primarily started in four districts, Puri, Cuttack, Dhenkanal and Keonjhar.

The progress of working of OMFED in Orissa, an open institution for undertaking dairy development activities in the State is depicted in Table 3.10. It is pertinent to note that the dairy development in Orissa passed through two phases since its date of operation i.e. 1980 to 1985-86 (OF-II) and 1987-88 to 1990-91 the first four years of operation OF-II project in Orissa.

The number of cooperatives increased from 52 to 270 during 1980-81 to 1985-86 and during 1990-91 it was 610, increasing 11.7 times during past 10 years and in the same time membership of cooperatives increased 14 times from 3.3 thousand (1980-81) to 46.2 thousand in 1990-91.

Animal covered under health and AI Services increased form 4.5 thousand (in 1980-81 to 85.7 thousand in 1980-91 which is more than 19 times. Milk procurement raised from 771.2 thousand kg in 1980-81 to 14891 thousand kg in 1990-

**Table 3.10 : Performance of OMFED**

| Sl. No. | Indicators | 1980-81 | 1985-86 | 1987-88 | 1990-91 | 2002-03 |
|---|---|---|---|---|---|---|
| 0 | 1 | 2 | 3 | 4 | 5 | 6 |
| 1. | Functional of Dairy Cooperative Societies (Cumulative) | 52 (100.00) | 270 (519) | 390 (950) | 610 (1172) | 1015 (1952) |
| 2. | Membership of Dairy Cooperatives (in '000 ltr.) | 3.3 (100.00) | 15.9 (48.2) | 24.2 (733) | 46.2 (1400) | 115.0 (3485) |
| 3. | Milk Procurement (in '000 Nøs.) | 771.2 (100.00) | 5245.0 (680) | 9403.03 (1219) | 14891.5 (1931) | 10600 (1374) |
| 4. | Animals covered Under Animal Health and Artificial Insemination (in '000 Nos.) | 4.5 (100.00) | 43.0 (956) | 61.0 (1356) | 85.7 (1904) | 112.7 (2504) |
| 5. | Milk markted by District Milk Unions and Federations (in '000 ltr.) | 939.7 (100.00) | 6760.5 (719) | 11696.6 (1245) | 24434.2 (2600) | |
| 6. | Ghee marketed (in '000 kg) | 7.4 (100.00) | 81.6 (1103) | 89.7 (1212) | 145.0 (1959) | 387.7 (5239) |

| | | | | | | |
|---|---|---|---|---|---|---|
| 7. | Sweetened Flavoured Milk Marketed | 2.3 (100.00) | 67.0 (291.3) | 272.2 (11835) | 319.7 (13900) | |
| 8. | Cattle Feed Markted (In '000 MT) | 0.2 (100.00) | 3.3 (1650) | 7.4 (3700) | 11.7 (5850) | 9.3 (4550) |

Figures in parentheses represent index of growth by taking 1980-81 as base year.
**Source:** 10th Annual Report 2002-03, OMFED, Bhubaneswar economic survey (2003-04).

91, 19.3 times increase over the period. The AI the same time milk marketing by OMFED increased 26 times from 939.7 thousand litres in 1980-81 to 94434.2 thousand litres in 1980-91. the marketing of ghee also has been increasing from 7.4 thousand kg. In 1980-81 to 145.0 thousand kg in 1990-91 is more than 19 and half times increase over the period. Sweetened flavoured OMFED milk in bottles increased 139 times i.e. from 2.3 thousand bottles in 1980-81 to 319.7 thousand bottles in 199-91 the cattle feed marketing also increased from 0.2 thousand MT from 1980-81 to 11.2 thousand MTs in 1990-91 i.e., 56 fold increase over the 10 years of period.

In addition to various government programmes to alleviate poverty and assured employment and income for rural poor such as Small Farmers Development Agency (SFDA), Marginal Farmers and Agricultural Labourers Development Agency (MFAL), Integrated Rural Development Programme (IRDP), Drought Prone Area Programme (DPAP) etc. providing milch animals under Area Development Approach for Poverty Termination (ADAPT) launched by Government of Orissa in Nuwapara (Kalahandi) district from 1988-89 was a special integrated Programme of dairy development through which rural poverty of the area can be eradicated and improvement in the conditions of rural poor can be achieved.

The programme of dairy development depends on our bovine stock continued by the cattle and buffaloes. The main purpose of rearing goat and sheep has been meat and not milk. So, note on bovine stock is followed.

It is also pertinent to note here that from above analysis of Secondary facts and figures it can easily be concluded that the dairy development has been inadequate in Orissa as against the requirement for milk and milk products. So efforts should be made to accelerate the dairy development in Orissa, acceptable to its villagers and viable from the economic point of view. Before taking any decision a cursory look at the rural scenario will reflect the issues and problems associated with the dairy development.

## TECHNOLOGY MISSION

The Government of Orissa prepared a proposal (March 1988) to commence technology mission activities for dairy development the main objectives were: (a) to accelerate the pace of increase in rural income and development through dairy (b) to accelerate the pace of application and adoption of modern technology to improve productivity, and to reduce costs of operation and to ensure greater availability of milk and dairy products, and (c) to coordinate operation Flood II programmes with State Government animal Husbandry and Dairy programmes.

Under this programme, the society areas are covered by veterinary Assts surgeons by visiting once in a fortnight during their regular tours for rendering veterinary checks, treatments and pregnancy diagnosis some of the new technologies like area treated for straw, fodder development, propagation of urea molasses blocks are also implemented with close coordination with the State Government.

### Orissa Women's Dairy Project

In order to ensure the overall development and well-being of rural based women from all walks of life, since 1996, OMFED has been implementing "Orissa Women's Dairy Project" in the undivided districts of Cuttack, Puri, Dhenkanal, Sambalpur, Ganjam, Balasore, and Bhadrak with Financial support from women and child development department, Ministry of Human Resource Development, Government of India. The main objective of this programme is to empower and self reliant to rural women belonging to SC/ST communities, asset less families, and families below poverty line. By the end of 2002-03, 679 dairy cooperatives have been formed with total membership of 57,791 and 39,3453 kg of milk per day is procured from these women dairy cooperatives (Government of Orissa, 2003-04).

A perusal of the aforesaid analysis brings into light that during plan period, efforts have been continuously undertaken for dairy development in Orissa. The growth of milk production also presents an increasing trend. However, compared to national level, there has been low production in milk as revealed in our study. It is heartening to note that OMFED has made significant progress in the production of milk and milk-products. However, in the context of rural poverty, there is an imperative to intensify dairying and milk production in the State.

# 4

# Profile of the Study Area

Profile of the study area in terms of consumption, production, infrastructure, employment pattern, topography, climatic conditions, its location etc. bears intimate link while discussing dairying and its impact on rural development. This chapter ventures at examining the above facts by analysing the specified indicators, which are as follows:

## LOCATION OF THE SAMPLE DISTRICTS

Ganjam and Puri two adjoining districts close to Bay of Bengal are located at the coastal plain agro-climatic zone of Orissa. Geographically, Ganjam is located at 80°9' to 85°11' East longitude and 19°0' to 20°17' North latitude whereas Puri lies in 84°29' to 86°25' East longitude and 19°28' to 20°35' North latitude. The geographical area of the two districts stand at 1176,000 hectares which is 7.55 % of the geographical area of the state. Alluvial soil, white sandy soil, red laterite and alkaline soil constitute the soil structure of the sample districts. The mean temperature varies between 42° in summer and 12° in winter. Humid and sub-humid types of climatic conditions prevail in both the districts.

## DEMOGRAPHIC PARTICULARS

Demographically speaking, in both the districts the sex ratio is not in favour of females. However, in Puri district females are comparatively more disadvantageous than Ganjam district on the grounds that the sex ratio in Puri district remains 968 against 998 in Ganjam district according to the 2001 census. More than 80 per cent of the population reside in rural areas and the incidence of rural population in Puri is 86.42 per cent which is higher than the corresponding figure in Ganjam district. Population density in both the districts is higher than the state average. The population density in Ganjam and Puri is 385 and 432 respectively (See Table 4.1).

**Table 4.1 : Demographic Particulars of the Selected Districts**

| Sl. No. | Demographic Particulars | Ganjam | Puri | Orissa |
|---|---|---|---|---|
| 1. | Total Population (in '000) | 3161 | 1502 | 36804 |
| 2. | Male | 1583 | 763 | 18660 |
| 3. | Female | 1579 | 739 | 18144 |
| 4. | % of Rural Population to Total Population | 82.40 | 86.42 | 85.01 |
| 5. | No. of Females Per Thousand Males | 998 | 968 | 972 |
| 6. | Population Density | 385 | 432 | 236 |

**Source**: Government of Orissa, 2005

## WORK FORCE PARTICIPATION

The workforce in the selected districts is ana lysed on the basis of the census data. The census classification of workforce is done on the basis of total workers, main workers, marginal workers, cultivators, agricultural labourers and non-workers the details of the workforce participation in the districts under study is shown in Table 4.2.

From Table 4.2 it is found that total workers and marginal workers constitute around 65 per cent of the total population in Orissa which is 67.6 per cent in Ganjam district and 54.98 in Puri district. Incidence of marginal workers in Ganjam districts is also found higher than Puri district and the overall situation in Orissa. In this background workforce participation rate in Ganjam district is better.

**Table 4.2 : Workforce Participation in the Selected Districts (2001 Census)**

| Sl. No. | Type of Workers | Ganjam (in '000) | Puri (in '000) | Orissa (in '000) |
|---|---|---|---|---|
| 1. | Total Workers | 1305<br>(41.60) | 451<br>(30.1) | 14273<br>(38.88) |
| 2. | Main Workers | 817<br>(26.0) | 373<br>(24.88) | 9573<br>(26.07) |
| 3. | Marginal Workers | 484<br>(15.5) | 78<br>(5.20) | 4700<br>(12.80) |
| 4. | Cultivators | 323<br>(10.29) | 158<br>(10.54) | 4238<br>(11.54) |
| 5. | Agricultural Labourers | 502<br>(16.0) | 113<br>(7.53) | 5001<br>(13.62) |
| | Total Population | 3137<br>(100.00) | 1499<br>(100.00) | 36707<br>(100.00) |

**Source:** Government of Orissa, 2005

## THE SOCIO-ECONOMIC STATUS OF THE SAMPLE DISTRICTS

The socio-economic status of the sample districts is expressed in terms of DDP per capita, teacher-student ratio, literacy rate, female literacy, percentage of safe delivery, percentage age of children completely immunised, IMR and mean years of schooling. The behaviour of these selected indicators in two districts is highlighted in Table 4.3.

The District Domestic Product (DDP) per capita (Rs.) in the two districts under study is less than the state Domestic product in Orissa. The State Domestic Product in Orissa is Rs. 5,264 as against the DDP of Rs. 5,013, and Rs. 4,933 in Ganjam and Puri respectively. The teacher student ratio in primary Schools stands at 0.105 and 0.106 respectively in Ganjam and Puri which is 0.018 in Orissa.

**Table 4.3 : Secio-economic Indicators in the Sample District**

| Sl. No. | Selected Socio-Economic Indicators | Ganjam | Puri | Orissa |
|---|---|---|---|---|
| 1. | District Domestic Product Per Capita | 5013 | 4933 | 5264 |
| 2. | Teacher-Student Ratio (Primary Schools) | 0.015 | 0.016 | 0.018 |
| 3. | Literacy Rate (%) | 60.77 | 77.96 | 63.08 |
| 4. | Female Literacy (%) 2001 | 47.7 | 67.8 | 50.97 |
| 5. | % of Safe Delivery | 35.3 | 54.6 | 48.9 |
| 6. | % of Children Completely Immunised | 37.5 | 60.5 | N.A. |
| 7. | IMR | 107 | 73 | 97 |
| 8. | Mean Years of Schooling | 3.94 | 3.75 | 2.42 |

**Source:** Orissa Human Development Report, 2004.

So far as literacy rate is concerned, it is higher in Puri in comparison to Ganjam (60.77%) and the state figure i.e. overall literacy in Orissa, which is 63.08%. Female literacy also performs well in Puri District in comparison to the corresponding figures in Ganjam in Orissa. The Female literacy rate in Puri is 67.8 per cent as against 47.7 in Ganjam and 50.97, the overall literacy rate in Orissa.

Similarly, the socio-economic indicators, more specifically the human development indicators like prevalence of safe delivery, percentage of children completely immunised Infant Mortality Rate (IMR), mean years of schooling etc. are favourable in Puri district in comparison to Ganjam District and all Orissa picture. For instance, IMR in Ganjam district which is 107 is much higher than Puri District.

## PERFORMANCE OF AGRICULTURE

The performance of agriculture in the study area is examined by considering selected agricultural indicators as sown in Table 4.4.

**Table 4.4 : Agricultural Scenario in the Sample Districts (2002-03)**

| Sl. No. | Selected Agriculture Indicators | Ganjam | Puri | Orissa |
|---|---|---|---|---|
| 1. | Cropping Intensity | 144 | 165 | 138 |
| 2. | Irrigation Intensity | 114.5 | 130.4 | 137.3 |
| 3. | Net Irrigated Area (in '000 ha) | 179.12 | 62.93 | 1246.81 |
| 4. | Consumption of Fertiliser | 58 | 39 | 39 |
| 5. | Net Irrigated Area as % to Nsa | 46.0 | 43.4 | 22.0 |
| 6. | HYV Paddy as % to total paddy | 78.7 | 75.0 | 70.7 |
| 7. | Summer Paddy as % to total paddy | 0.0 | 11.0 | 4.2 |
| 8. | Average Yield of Paddy (Q./ha) | 866 | 873 | 759 |
| 9. | Average Yield for foodgrains | 740 | 742 | 675 |

**Source:** Complied from Agriculture Census Orissa and Economic Survey, 2004

It is revealed from the statement that cropping intensity and irrigation intensity both are higher in the district in comparison to Ganjam district. Even though, the net irrigated area in Ganjam district is more than double the net irrigated area in Puri district, lower cropping intensity and irrigation intensity of the district indicates lower agriculture practises among the farmers. The net irrigated area as a percentage to the net sown area stands marginally higher in Ganjam district.

Consumption of chemical fertiliser expressed in terms of kg/heactre is higher in Ganjam district than Puri and the overall picture in Orissa. HYV paddy as a percentage to total paddy is higher in Ganjam district. Higher consumption of chemical fertiliser is attributed to higher proportion of HYV paddy to total paddy. On the other hand, summer paddy as a percentage to total paddy is almost non-existent in Ganjam district and it is 11.0 per cent in Puri district. The overall performance of summer paddy in Orissa is only 4.2 per cent. Yield rate of paddy (QHL/hectare) is marginally higher in Puri district than Ganjam district. Similarly, with respect to average yield of food-grains, Puri is again better than Ganjam district and the overall picture of the State.

From the above analysis, it follows that, the agricultural practices in Puri district is better than Ganjam district.

## ANIMAL HUSBANDRY

Next to agriculture, animal husbandry is the most important economic activity in rural areas. The performance of animal husbandry in the sample districts is analysed on the basis of selected animal husbandry indicators. The performance of different indicators is shown in Table 4.5.

The livestock aid centres in Ganjam district is more than Puri. Buffaloes population in Ganjam district is around double the buffaloes in Puri district. The cattle population consisting of crossbred and indigenous cattle in Ganjam and Puri district stand at 8,41,661 and 4,61,992 respectively. Among the total cows, crossbred cows account 31.12 and 22.69 in Ganjam and Puri respectively. However, in absolute terms, the total number of crossbred cows in Puri are three times higher than the crossbred cows in Ganjam district. The total number of sheep, goat and poultry population jointly stand at 1805174 which is more than 4 times higher than corresponding figure at 463302 in Puri district.

**Table 4.5 : Selected Indictors on Animal Husbandry**

| Sl. No. | Animal Husbandry Indicators | Ganjam | Puri | Orissa |
|---|---|---|---|---|
| 1. | Livestock aid centres | 246 | 145 | 2939 |
| 2. | Buffaloes (Nos.) | 131305 | 16649 | 1388024 |
| 3. | Cattle: | | | |
| | —Crossbred | 25405 | 85417 | 869615 |
| | —Indigenous | 816256 | 376575 | 12898275 |
| 4. | Cows: | | | |
| | —Crossbred | 18822 | 68116 | 624345 |
| | —Indigenous | 424025 | 204858 | 58881142 |
| 5. | Sheep | 145914 | 75041 | 1779367 |
| 6. | Goat | 218370 | 120128 | 5879723 |
| 7. | Poultry | 1427292 | 266074 | 1756557 |
| 8. | Pig | 13571 | 2059 | 601917 |

**Source:** Government of Orissa, 2005.

However, in Orissa, cows and buffaloes are only treated as milch animals and present policies are aimed at increasing the number of cross-bred cows. In this light, the position of Ganjam and Puri is commendable.

## MILK, EGG, MEAT AND FISH PRODUCTION

In the latest agricultural policies, agro-diversification constitutes the basic thrust for improving the agricultural performance. Thus, simultaneous improvement in the production of milk, egg, meat, and fish along with increased agricultural production is known as agro-diversification. With a view to analyse, agro-diversification, the production figures of milk, egg, meat and fish for the year 2004-05 is presented in Table 4.6.

From Table 4.7, it is found that Ganjam and Puri jointly account around 16 per cent of the state milk production. Except egg production, the production of milk, meat and fish is higher in Puri district in comparison to Ganjam district.

**Table 4.6 : Production of Milk, Egg, meat, and fish in the Selected Districts**

| Sl. No. | Items of Production | Ganjam | Puri | Orissa |
|---|---|---|---|---|
| 1. | Milk (in '000 mt) | 69 | 80 | 941 |
| 2. | Egg (in Million No.) | 168 | 9 | 904 |
| 3. | Meat (in mt) | 1475 | 1589 | 44725 |
| 4. | Fish (in mt) | 27498 | 36046 | 282129 |

**Source:** Government of Orissa, 2005, Directorate of Economics and Statistics, *District Statistical Handbook,* 2001.

## INCIDENCE OF POVERTY

The basic issue of all rural development programmes is to improve the socio-economic status of the marginalised and vulnerable sections of the community and ultimately ameliorating rural poverty. The present status of poverty in the two districts is presented in terms of head count of index, the incidence of poverty and Monthly Per Capita Consumption Expenditure (MPCE). The performance of these two indicators on the basis of NSS 55th Round Survey (Hann & Dubey, 2004) is presented in Table 4.79.

**Table 4.7 : Incidence of Poverty in the Selected Districts**

| Sl. No. | Poverty Indicators | Ganjam | Puri | Orissa |
|---|---|---|---|---|
| 1. | Head Count Ratio | 40.73 | 20.09 | 48.14 |
| 2. | MPCE (Rs.) | 383.73 | 447.31 | 372.95 |

*Source*: Government of Orissa, 2005.

It is found that the incidence of poverty in Ganjam and Puri district is 40.73 and 20.09 respectively. Thus with regard to the incidence of poverty, Ganjam district is having higher incidence of poverty which is twice the incidence of poverty in Puri district. The MPCE in Puri is Rs. 447, which is higher than the MPCE of Ganjam district. The incidence of poverty considering the indicators like Head Count Ratio and MPCE is given in Table 4.7.

## ANIMAL HEALTH INSTITUTIONS

The animal health institutions in the study area is presented in Table 4.8 it is found that there are one cattle and buffalo farm, three veterinary poly clinics, 34 veterinary dispensaries, 242 first aid centres and one disease diagnostic centre in Ganjam district. On the other hand in Puri district there are one liquid nitrogen plant, four veterir.ary poly clinics, 451 veterinary dispensaries and 248 veterinary first aid centres.

**Table 4.8 : Artificial Insemination and Animal Health Institutions in Orissa**

| Sl. No. | Particulars | Ganjam | Puri | Orissa |
|---|---|---|---|---|
| 1. | Cattle Buffalo Farms | 1 | - | 13 |
| 2. | Liquid Nitrogen Plants | 0 | 1 | 10 |
| 3. | Veterinary Poly-clinics/hospitals | 3 | 4 | 58 |
| 4. | Veterinary Dispensaries | 34 | 45 | 451 |
| 5. | Veterinary First-aid Centres | 242 | 278 | 2831 |
| 6. | Disease Diagnostic Centres | 1 | - | 5 |

**Source:** Department of Animal Husbandry and Dairying, Government of India, 1993-94.

## LAND UTILISATION PATTERN

The land utilisation pattern in Ganjam and Puri district is discussed on the basis of 10-fold classification which is presented in Table 4.9.

**Table 4.9 : Land Utilisation Pattern in the Selected Districts**

| Sl. No. | Particulars | Ganjam | Puri | Orissa |
|---|---|---|---|---|
| 1. | Geographical Area ('000 ha) | 870 | 306 | 15541 |
| 2. | Forest Area | 308 | 328 | 5534 |
| 3. | Net Area Sown | 360 | 469 | 6303 |
| 4. | Permanent Pasture | 24 | 45 | 635 |
| 5. | Trees and Groves | 29 | 25 | 867 |
| 6. | Cultivable Waste | 11 | 27 | 487 |
| 7. | Uncultivable Waste | 0 | 43 | 541 |
| 8. | Current Fallow | 38 | 17 | 149 |
| 9. | Other Fallow | 8 | 25 | 243 |
| 10. | Land-used of Land Agricultural Purposes | 45 | 67 | 781 |

**Source:** Director of Economics and Statistics, Government of Orissa, 2005.

It is found that Ganjam and Puri jointly account 7.57 per cent of the geographical area, 11.6 of the forest area, 10.9 of the pasture area, and 14.4 per cent of the agricultural lands of the state. Further, it is found that permanent pasture is higher in Puri district in relation to Ganjam district.

## RAINFALL SITUATION

The rainfall situation in the two districts under study is analysed on the basis of normal rainfall normal number of days of rainfall. The normal rainfall and normal rainy days in Ganjam and Puri district is less than the normal figures prevailing in the State (See Table 4.10 for details).

## HOUSING PARTICULARS

Housing particulars in the district are analysed on the basis of the census data 2001. For analysing housing particulars, variable like number of dwelling rooms, percentage of married couples having independent sleeping rooms, source of drinking water, source of lighting, sanitation, type of fuel used for cooking etc. are presented in Table 4.11.

**Table 4.10 : Rain Fall indicators in the Selected Districts**

| Sl. No. | Rainfall Indicators | Ganjam | Puri | Orissa |
|---|---|---|---|---|
| 1. | Normal Rainfall | 1295.6 | 1449.1 | 1502.6 |
| 2. | Normal Rainy | 65.4 | 69.7 | 73.4 |

**Source:** Orissa Agricultural Statistics, 2004

**Table 4.11 : Housing Particulars in the Selected Districts**

| Sl. No. | Dwelling Rooms for Households | Ganjam | Puri | Orissa |
|---|---|---|---|---|
| 0 | 1 | 2 | 3 | 4 |
| 1. | No. of Exclusive Room | 1.63 | 1.07 | 1.64 |
| 2. | One Room | 27.08 | 35.37 | 36.61 |
| 3. | Two Rooms | 33.20 | 33.73 | 36.98 |
| 4. | Three and more rooms | 38.09 | 29.83 | 24.77 |
| 5. | Percentage of Married Couples Having Independent Sleeping Rooms | 54.31 | 73.71 | 66.15 |
| 6. | *Drinking Water Sources*: | | | |
| | Tap | 11.11 | 7.36 | 8.73 |
| | Hand Pump | 16.84 | 28.17 | 28.47 |
| | Tube Well | 31.24 | 42.78 | 26.98 |
| | Wells | 33.52 | 14.74 | 28.55 |
| | Others | 7.28 | 7.05 | 7.26 |
| 7. | *Sources of Lighting*: | | | |
| | Electricity | 33.70 | 30.61 | 26.93 |
| | Kerosene | 65.18 | 68.24 | 72.10 |
| | Other Sources | 0.57 | 0.57 | 0.53 |
| | No Lighting | 0.56 | 0.58 | 0.46 |

*(contd.)*

| 0 | 1 | 2 | 3 | 4 |
|---|---|---|---|---|
| 8. | *Sanitation Bathroom:* | 30.94 | 10.50 | 10.51 |
| | Latrine | 37.51 | 17.67 | 14.89 |
| | Drainage | 38.50 | 30.16 | 20.74 |
| 9. | *Fuel for Cooking* : | | | |
| | Firewood | 49.44 | 46.29 | 69.44 |
| | LPG | 20.97 | 3.93 | 5.22 |
| | Others | 29.23 | 49.54 | 25.08 |
| | No Cooking | 0.36 | 0.24 | 0.26 |

**Source:** Census Reports, 2001.

## DWELLING ROOM

From Table 4.11 it is found that around 73 per cent of the households in Orissa have one-two dwelling rooms, which is found lower in Ganjam (60.28%) and Puri (69.10%) districts. However households having more than three living rooms are found higher in both the districts under study. Households without and exclusive living room are found between 1 and two per cent.

### Independent Sleeping Rooms

Form Table 4.11 it is further evident that around 34 per cent of the married couples are not having independent sleeping rooms. The corresponding figure is around 46 per cent in Ganjam district and 37 per cent in Puri district.

### Pattern of Drinking Water

For drinking water purposes, around 55 per cent of the households In Orissa depend on hand pumps and tube wells. This type of dependence is marginally higher in Puri District and lower in Ganjam district. Around 11 per cent of the households in Ganjam district use tap water for drinking purposes which is comparatively lower in Puri and overall pattern in Orissa.

## Source of Lighting

Broadly, there are two sources of lighting such as kerosene and electricity more than 65 per cent of the households still use kerosene as the main source of lighting. Only 27 per cent of the households in Orissa depend on electricity as the source of lighting. The corresponding figures in Ganjam and Puri district are slightly better.

## Sanitation

For assessing sanitation, access to bathroom, latrine and drainage are examined. It is found that 30.94 per cent of the households are having access to bathroom, 37.51 per cent of the households have access to latrine and 38.5 per cent of the households have access to drainage in Ganjam district. On the other hand, the households having access to latrine (17.67%), access to bathroom (10.50%) and access to drainage (30.16%) in Puri district are found as per Table 4.11. With respect to sanitation the districts under study are better than the overall picture of the state.

## Fuel used for Cooking

It is revealed from Table 4.11 that, around 50 per cent of the households in Ganjam district and 46 per cent of the households in Puri district use firewood for cooking purposes as against around 70 per cent of the households in Orissa. Similarly, around 21 per cent of the households in Ganjam district use LPG gas for cooking purposes which is only 3.93 per cent in Puri and 5.22 per cent in Orissa. The use of other traditional fuels like dung cakes, agriculture wastes twigs etc. stands higher in Puri district.

# POSSESSION OF CONSUMER DURABLES

The performance of rural development in the two districts has been studied considering the degree of concentration of physical assets and financial assets. It is found that around 24 per cent of the households in both the districts are availing banking services, which is roughly same to the overall performance of the state. The physical assets (consumer durables) as possessed by the sample households of the two districts are portrayed in Table 4.12.

**Table 4.12 : Possession of Consumer Durables in the Selected Districts**

| Sl. No. | Particulars | Ganjam | Puri | Orissa |
|---|---|---|---|---|
| 1 | % of Households Availing Banking Services | 24.21 | 23.37 | 24.21 |
| 2. | *Availability of Assets* (% of Households) | | | |
| | Radio and Transistor | 19.23 | 30.57 | 23.66 |
| | Television | 17.89 | 17.08 | 15.49 |
| | Bicycle | 39.77 | 55.78 | 51.96 |
| | Telephone | 4.51 | 13.35 | 3.95 |
| | Scooter/Motorcycle | 7.24 | 23.70 | 7.86 |
| | Car/Jeepi/Vans | 0.95 | 3.71 | 1.08 |

**Source:** Census Report 2001.

The possession of other consumer durables like radio, bicycle, telephone, scooter, motor-cycle, car/jeep/van etc. is found higher in Puri district. Even the performance of Puri district is better than the overall picture in the state. In this background, it is inferred that the state of rural development is better in Puri district than in Ganjam district.

## FOOD-GRAIN PRODUCTION

Time series analysis of data on food-grain production, area under food-grain production and yield rate suggests that over years food-grains production has increased in both the districts. However, area under food-grain production has reduced in both the districts. Though yield rate of food-grains shows continuously increasing trend, but, yield rate of food-grains in Ganjam is found better than Puri District (See Table 4.13).

**Table 4.13 : Trends of Food-grain Production in the Selected Districts**

| Sl. No. | Year | Ganjam | | | Puri | | |
|---|---|---|---|---|---|---|---|
| | | Food production ('000 mt) | Area under food-grain ('000 ha) | Yield rate (kg/ ha) | Food production ('000 mt) | Area under food-grain ('000 ha) | Yield rate (kg/ ha) |
| 1. | 1975-76 | 570.9 | 620.6 | 920.0 | 533.4 | 609.7 | 870.0 |
| 2. | 1980-81 | 647.9 | 701.1 | 920.0 | 556.2 | 689.7 | 810.0 |
| 3. | 1985-86 | 729.6 | 653.3 | 1117.0 | 723.3 | 643.1 | 1125.0 |
| 4. | 1990-91 | 707.5 | 715.2 | 989.0 | 520.4 | 567.9 | 916.0 |
| 5. | 1993-94 | 857.5 | 699.9 | 1225.0 | 820.4 | 614.3 | 1336.0 |
| 6. | 1998-99 | 710.4 | 593.2 | 1278.5 | 674.9 | 589.9 | 1156.0 |

**Source:** Orissa Agricultural Statistics, 1998-99.

## 4.16 FOREST COVERAGE

Forest coverage bears an important linkage with dairying on the ground that it provides natural fodder to cattle population. From Table 4.14, it is evident that forest area constitutes 30.21 per cent of the geographical area in Orissa which is 24.81 per cent in Ganjam District and only 4.06 per cent in Puri District. Though dense forests and open forests in Ganjam district account around 20 times and 15 times of the dense and open forest areas of Puri respectively, Still mangrove type of forest are not found in both the coastal districts (Table 4.14).

## SAMPLE VILLAGES

Profile of the sample villages have been explained by considering the type of work participation and occupational structure in the sample villages. The type of work and the occupational structure in the sample villages are mentioned in Table 4.15 and Table 4.16 respectively.

**Table 4.14 : Forest Coverage in the Selected Districts**

| Sl. No. | Type of Forest Coverage (in ha) | Ganjam | Puri | Orissa |
|---|---|---|---|---|
| 1. | Dense Forest | 1215 | 63 | 26073 |
| 2. | Open Forest | 945 | 61 | 20745 |
| 3. | Mangrove Forest | - | - | 215 |
| 4. | Total Forest | 2160 | 124 | 47003 |
| 5. | Forest Area as % to the Geographical Area | 24.81 | 4.06 | 30.21 |

**Source:** Forest Survey of India, 1999

As per Table 4.15, among the sample villages, highest proportion of total workers are found at Gopalpur Sasan (42.2) followed by Amrutulu (32.3), Dura-Bahadurpeta (31.6), and other villages where proportionate share of working population in less man 30 present. It is observed that proportionate share of working population in Puri is less then the proportionate share of working population in Ganjam. On the other hand, among all the sample village the proportionate share of non workers in found maximum at Denuan (73.1%) located in Puri district and minimum at Gopalpursasan situated in Ganjam district.

Table 4.16 shows that the proportionate share agriculture dependent population varies in the range of around 60-80 per cent in the sample villages striated in Ganjam district as against around 18-75 per cent in Ganjam district. Among all the villages under study highest proportion of agricultural labours around 80 per cent are found at Jankia village in Puri district and minimum at around 18 per cent at Rangeilunda village. Because Rangeilunda is very close to Berhampur and favourably located around the nearby townships of Gopalpur, Berhampur University and Golabandha Cantonment a big chunk of the agricultural land have been converted into construction sites. As a matter of fact, the bonafide agricultural workers and cultivators of this village are mainly entering into dairying activities. Similarly, in Dura-Bahadurpeta, another sample village in Ganjam district, due to its proximity

**Table 4.15 : Total Population and Workers in the Sample Villages**

| Sl. | Particulars | Ganjam | | | | | |
|---|---|---|---|---|---|---|---|
| | | Konisi | | Suruda | | Nimapada | |
| | | Dura-Bahadurpeta | Rangeilunda | Amrutulu | Gopalpur Sasan | Denuan | Jagdeshwar-pur |
| 1. | Total Population | 3715 | 2275 | 2000 | 1020 | 3811 | 698 |
| | | (100.0) | (100.0) | (100.0) | (100.0) | (100.0) | (100.0) |
| 2. | Total Worker | 1175 | 625 | 646 | 430 | 1025 | 209 |
| | | (31.6) | (27.5) | (32.3) | (42.2) | (26.9) | (29.9) |
| 3. | Total Main Workers | 905 | 549 | 508 | 244 | 893 | 186 |
| | | (24.4) | (24.1) | (25.4) | (23.9) | (23.4) | (26.6) |
| 4. | Total Marginal Workers | 270 | 76 | 138 | 186 | 132 | 23 |
| | | (7.3) | (3.3) | (6.9) | (18.2) | (3.5) | (3.3) |

N.B. : Figures in parentheses are percentage to total population.

**Table 4.16 : Distribution of Total Workers in the Sample Villages According to Major Occupation**

| Sl. | Particulars | Ganjam | | | | |
|---|---|---|---|---|---|---|
| | | Konisi | | Suruda | | Nimapada |
| | | Dura-Bahadurpeta | Rangeilunda | Amrutulu | Gopalpur Sasan | Denuan |
| 1. | Total Non-Workers | 2540 (68.4) | 1650 (72.5) | 1354 (67.7) | 590 (57.8) | 2786 (73.1) |
| 2. | Cultivators | 155 (13.2) | 20 (3.2) | 394 (61.0) | 62 (14.4) | 458 (47.7) |
| 3. | Agricultural Labourers | 311 (26.5) | 89 (14.2) | 101 (15.6) | 162 (37.7) | 226 (22.0) |
| 4. | Household Industry | 29 (2.5) | 12 (1.9) | 16 (2.5) | 3 (0.7) | 64 (6.2) |
| 5. | Other Workers | 680 (57.8) | 504 (80.7) | 135 (20.9) | 203 (47.2) | 277 (27.0) |
| 6. | Total Workers | 1175 (100.0) | 625 (100.0) | 646 (100.0) | 430 (100.0) | 1025 (100.0) |

N. B. : Figures in parentheses are percentage to total population.

to Berhampur and National Highway-5 , most of the agricultural lands have been acquired for the Tata Steel Project site. For the same reason cited above the existing farmers is taking dairying as the main avocation. In all other sample villages, except Denuan at Nimapara block, the incidence of exclusive agricultural dependence is very high because of the implementation of landholding consolidation and irrigation provisions.

The foregoing illustrations make it clear that Ganjam and Puri, two coastal districts are having immense potentiality for dairying. The selected blocks and villages have their scope for boosting dairying.

# 5

# Economics of Dairying among the Sample Households

The present chapter is an attempt to explain the economics of dairying among the sample households. The economics of dairying at household level are analysed by examining the parameters like stock of animals in the sample area, average size of milch animal, type of milk production, consumption and sales; Besides, the economic traits of cattle are studied in the light of age at first calving lactation length, dry period, calving interval Type of feeding practices and milk marketing system of the sample households are also analysed to understand a better perspective as regard to the economics of dairying. In the last section of this chapter, constraints in dairy development are discussed.

## BOVINE STOCK

The programme of dairy development largely depends on the bovine stock of the sample households which consists of bullock, non-descript cows, crossbred cows/calves, buffaloes/ calves, goats/and sheep. Out of 1114 animal stock in Ganjam district 881 (71.21%) animals among the dairy households and 259 animals (21.71%) among the non-dairy households are found. Major proportion of the bovine stock of sample households in this district consist of bullocks (24.56%) followed by non-descript cows (15.61%) crossbred cows (5.08%), buffaloes (5.08%) goats (5.43%) and sheep (0.32%). On the other hand, crossbred cows constitute a major share among the animal stock of the sample households in Puri district and the proportionate share of crossbred cows in the animal stock is around 26% followed by bullock and non-descript cows [(see Table 5.1(a)].

As per Table 5.1(a) the mean bovine stock of the dairy households, in Ganjam district stands at 8.81 as against the mean bovine 2.59 among the non-dairy households. As against the mean stock of all animals at 5.77 among the dairy households in Puri district, the mean stock of animals among the non-dairy households is found at 1.42. Thus, the average stock of animals per dairy households as well as non-dairy households in Ganjam is higher than Puri district. However, the mean stock of crossbred cows is marginally higher in Puri district.

Further distribution of livestock among the dairy and non-dairy households in both the districts under study are separately presented on the basis of operational landholdings in Table 5.1(b) and 5.1(c) respectively.

As per Table 5.1 (b), in Ganjam district the mean numbers of animals among dairy and non-dairy households are estimated to be 5.77 and 1.33 respectively. The mean number of animals among dairy households is found to be highest for small farmers which are 8.1 followed by large farmers (7.9), marginal farmers (4.02) and landless households (2.6). The mean livestock households among the non-dairy households consisting of large farmers, small farmers, marginal farmers, and landless labourers are found to be 4.25, 1.92, 0.88 and 0.37 respectively. Similarly, in Puri District [(See Table 5.1.(c)] the number of animals per dairy households is found at 9.0, which is 2.6 among non-dairy households. The mean number of animals among LFs, SFs, MFs, and LLs is 10.3, 9.0, 11.4 and 5.7 respectively among dairy households. The corresponding figures 3.9, 3.0, 1.2, 2.6 are found for LFs, SFs, MFs, and LLs respectively among the non-dairy households.

**Table 5.1(a) : Bovine Stock among the Sample Households**

| Sl. No. | Bovine Stock | Ganjam | | | | | |
|---|---|---|---|---|---|---|---|
| | | No. of Animals Among Dairy | Mean Animal Stock (Dairy (Dairy HHs | No. of Animals Among Non-Dairy HHs) | Mean Animal Stock (Non- HHs | Animal Stock All Households Dairy HHs | Mean Animal Stock of All HHs |
| 0 | 1 | 2 | 3 | 4 | 5 | 6 | 7 |
| 1. | Bullock | 148 (16.79) | 1.48 | 132 (50.96) | 1.32 | 280 (24.56) | 1.4 |
| 2. | Non-Descript Cows | 125 (14.18) | 1.25 | 53 (20.46) | 0.53 | 178 (15.61) | 0.89 |
| 3. | Calves | 88 (18.50) | 0.88 | 29 (11.19) | 0.29 | 117 (10.26) | 0.58 |
| 4. | Cross-bred Cows | 163 (18.50) | 1.63 | 6 (2.31) | 0.06 | 169 (14.82) | 0.84 |
| 5. | Calves | 130 (14.75) | 1.30 | 2 (0.77) | 0.02 | 132 (11.57) | 0.66 |
| 6. | He-Buffaloes | 36 (4.0) | 0.36 | 22 (8.49) | 0.22 | 58 (5.08) | 0.29 |

| | | | | | | | |
|---|---|---|---|---|---|---|---|
| 7. | She-Buffaloes | 53 (6.0) | 0.53 | 3 (1.15) | 0.03 | 58 (5.08) | 0.29 |
| 8. | Calves | 42 (2.49) | 0.22 | 1 (0.38) | 0.01 | 23 (2.01) | 011 |
| 9. | Goats | 51 (5.78) | 0.51 | 11 (4.27) | 0.11 | 62 (5.43) | 0.31 |
| 10. | Sheep | 65 (7.37) | 0.65 | - | - | 65 (7.48) | 0.32 |
| | Total | 88 (100.00) | 8.81 | 259 (100.00) | 2.59 | 1140 (100.00) | 5.7 |

*(contd.)*

| Sl. No. | Bovine Stock | Puri | | | | | |
|---|---|---|---|---|---|---|---|
| | | No. of Animals Among Dairy | Mean Animal Stock (Dairy (Dairy HHs | No. of Animals Among Non-Dairy HHs) | Mean Animal Stock (Non- HHs | Animal Stock All Households Dairy HHs | Mean Animal Stock of All HHs |
| 0 | 1 | 3 | 4 | 5 | 6 | 7 | 8 |
| 1. | Bullock | 110 (19.06) | 1.1 | 32 (28.07) | N.A. | N.A. | N.A. |
| 2. | Non-Descript Cows | 65 ((11.26) | 0.65 | 37 (32.45) | N.A. | N.A. | N.A. |
| 3. | Calves | 58 10.05) | 0.58 | 15 (13.15) | N.A. | N.A. | N.A. |
| 4. | Cross-bred Cows | 182 (31.54) | 1.82 | 2 (1.75) | N.A. | N.A. | N.A. |
| 5. | Calves | 126 (21.83) | 1.26 | - | N.A. | N.A. | N.A. |
| 6. | He-Buffaloes | 18 (3.11) | 0.18 | 12 (10.52) | N.A. | N.A. | N.A. |

| | | | | | | | |
|---|---|---|---|---|---|---|---|
| 7. | She-Buffaloes | 4<br>(0.69) | 0.04 | - | N.A. | N.A. | N.A. |
| 8. | Calves | 2<br>(0.34) | 0.02 | - | N.A. | N.A. | N.A. |
| 9. | Goats | 2<br>(0.34) | 0.02 | 11<br>(9.64) | N.A. | N.A. | N.A. |
| 10. | Sheep | 10<br>(1.73) | 0.10 | 5<br>(4.38) | N.A. | N.A. | N.A. |
| | Total | 577<br>(100.00) | 5.77 | 114<br>(100.00) | | | |

**Table 5.1(b) : Distribution of Sample Households according to Size of Operational Holding and Animal Stock (Ganjam District)**

| Sl. No. | Particulars | Dairy Households | | | | | Non-dairy Households | | | | |
|---|---|---|---|---|---|---|---|---|---|---|---|
| | | LL | MF | SF | LF | Total | LL | MF | SF | LF | Total |
| 0 | 1 | 2 | 3 | 4 | 5 | 6 | 7 | 8 | 9 | 10 | 11 |
| 1. | No. of Sample Households | 18 | 11 | 45 | 26 | 100 | - | 8 | 43 | 19 | 100 |
| 2. | No. of Bullocks | 2 | 6 | 82 | 58 | 148 | - | 14 | 72 | 46 | 132 |
| 3A. | Non-Descript Cows | 16 | 12 | 56 | 41 | 125 | 10 | 8 | 23 | 12 | 53 |
| 3.1 | Dry | 2 | 2 | 17 | 16 | 37 | 3 | 2 | 12 | 7 | 24 |
| 3.2 | In Milk | 14 | 10 | 39 | 25 | 88 | 7 | 6 | 11 | 5 | 29 |
| 3B. | Calves | 14 | 10 | 39 | 25 | 88 | 7 | 6 | 11 | 5 | 29 |
| 4A. | Crossbred cows | 18 | 26 | 69 | 50 | 163 | - | - | 2 | 4 | 6 |
| 4.1 | Dry | 4 | 10 | 11 | 8 | 33 | - | - | 1 | 3 | 4 |
| 4.2 | In Milk | 14 | 16 | 58 | 42 | 130 | - | - | 1 | 1 | 2 |
| 4B. | Calves | 14 | 16 | 58 | 42 | 130 | - | - | 1 | 1 | 2 |
| 5A. | He-buffaloes | - | 4 | 22 | 10 | 36 | - | - | 16 | 6 | 22 |
| 6A. | She-buffaloes | - | 5 | 32 | 16 | 53 | - | - | 3 | - | 3 |

| | | | | | | | | | | | |
|---|---|---|---|---|---|---|---|---|---|---|---|
| 6.1 | Dry | - | 1 | 7 | 3 | 1 | - | - | 2 | - | 2 |
| 6.2 | In Milk | - | 4 | 25 | 13 | 42 | - | - | 1 | - | 1 |
| 6.b | Calves | - | 4 | 25 | 13 | 42 | - | - | 1 | - | 1 |
| 7. | Goats | 26 | 19 | 6 | - | 51 | 4 | 7 | - | - | 11 |
| 8. | Sheep | 12 | 23 | 18 | 12 | 65 | - | - | - | - | - |
| | Total (2+3a+ 3b+4a+ 4b+5+6b+7+8) | 102 | 125 | 407 | 267 | 901 | 21 | 35 | 129 | 74 | 259 |
| | Mean Number of Animals | 57 | 11.4 | 9.0 | 10.3 | 9.0 | 2.6 | 1.2 | 3.0 | 3.9 | 2.6 |

**Table 5.1(c) : Distribution of Sample Households according to Size of Operational Holding and Animal Stock(Puri District)**

| Sl. No. | Particulars | Dairy Households | | | | | Non-dairy Households | | | | |
|---|---|---|---|---|---|---|---|---|---|---|---|
| | | LL | MF | SF | LF | Total | LL | MF | SF | LF | Total |
| 0 | 1 | 2 | 3 | 4 | 5 | 6 | 7 | 8 | 9 | 10 | 11 |
| 1. | No. of Sample Households | 10 | 44 | 38 | 8 | 100 | 8 | 42 | 26 | 4 | 80 |
| 2. | No. of Bullocks | 6 | 28 | 76 | 6 | 110 | - | 6 | 18 | 8 | 32 |
| 3.a | Non-descript Cows | 6 | 26 | 29 | 4 | 65 | 2 | 16 | 14 | 5 | 37 |
| 3.1 | Dry | 1 | 2 | 3 | 1 | 7 | 2 | 9 | 7 | 4 | 22 |
| 3.2 | In Milk | 5 | 24 | 26 | 3 | 58 | - | 7 | 7 | 1 | 15 |
| 3.b | Calves | 4 | 24 | 27 | 3 | 58 | - | 7 | 7 | 1 | 15 |
| 4.a | Crossbred Cows | 8 | 49 | 98 | 27 | 182 | 1 | - | 1 | 2 | 4 |
| 4.1 | Dry | 2 | 18 | 32 | 4 | 56 | 1 | - | - | 1 | 2 |
| 4.2 | In Milk | 6 | 31 | 66 | 23 | 126 | - | - | 1 | 1 | 2 |
| 4.b | Calves | 6 | 31 | 66 | 23 | 126 | - | - | 1 | 1 | 2 |
| 5.a | He-buffaloes | - | 10 | 8 | - | 18 | - | 6 | 6 | - | 12 |
| 6.a | She-buffaloes | - | 2 | 2 | - | 4 | - | - | - | - | - |

| | | | | | | | | | | | |
|---|---|---|---|---|---|---|---|---|---|---|---|
| 6.1 | Dry | - | 1 | 1 | - | 2 | - | - | - | - | - |
| 6.2 | In Milk | - | 1 | 1 | - | 2 | - | - | - | - | - |
| 6.b | Calves | - | 1 | 1 | - | 2 | - | - | - | - | - |
| 7. | Goats | 2 | - | - | - | 2 | - | - | - | - | - |
| 2.8 | Sheep | - | 6 | 4 | - | 10 | - | 2 | 3 | - | 5 |
| | Total (2+3A+3B+4A+ 4B+5+6B+7+8) | 26 | 177 | 311 | 63 | 577 | 3 | 37 | 50 | 17 | 107 |
| | Mean Number of | 2.6 | 4.02 | 8.1 | 7.9 | 5.77 | 0.37 | 0.88 | 1.92 | 4.25 | 1.32 |

From this analysis, it is inferred that the average number of animals in Puri district is found higher among both the categories of households. Among dairy households the mean holding animal is found highest among small farmers followed by large farmers and others in Ganjam district. On the other hand, marginal farmers dominate so far as livestock possession is concerned.

## STOCK OF MILCH ANIMALS

The stock of milch animals among the sample households is presented in Table 5.2 though in the bovine stock goats and sheep are reported, but these are not used for milking purposes in the study area. Thus, the status, of cows and buffaloes which are extensively treated as milch-animals are discussed.

Among the sample households in Ganjam district, there are 291 milch animals and 114 young stocks. The total value of all the milch animals and young stock are calculated at Rs. 21,13,950. The value per milch animal and young stock are calculated at Rs. 5,852 and Rs. 3,603 respectively. Similarly, there are 201 milch animals among the sample households in Puri District. The total value, average value per milch animals and the average value for young stock are found at Rs. 12,90,121, Rs. 6,418 and Rs. 3,478 respectively. The mean value of milch animals in Ganjam and Puri district are found at Rs. 5,852 and Rs. 6418 respectively. Similarly, the mean value of young stock is estimated at Rs. 3,603 and Rs. 3,478 in Ganjam and Puri respectively. It is observed that the mean value of milch animals in Puri stand higher in comparison to Ganjam. On the other hand the mean value of young stock in Ganjam district is found higher.

## INVESTMENT PATTERN

Farmer-category wise and milch animal wise the investment pattern is shown in Table 5.3. The mean investment being influenced by various coasts like sheds, equipments, and animals remain different for different/category of farmers. The overall mean investment in Ganjam district is highest

**Table 5.2 : Value of the Milch Animals among the Sample Households**

| Sl. No. | Category of Milch Animals | Ganjam | | | | | | Puri | | | | | |
|---|---|---|---|---|---|---|---|---|---|---|---|---|---|
| | | Milch Animal | | | Young Stock | | | Milch Animal | | | Young Stock | | |
| | | No. of Animals | Total Value | Value per Animal | No. of Animals | Total Value | Value Per Animal | No. of Animals | Total Value | Value Per Animal | No. of Animals | Total Value | Value Per Animal |
| 0 | 1 | 2 | 3 | 4 | 5 | 6 | 7 | 8 | 9 | 10 | 11 | 12 | 13 |
| 1. | Non-des. cows | 117 | 132132 | 1129 | 61 | 57119 | 936 | 73 | 93513 | 1281 | 29 | 30479 | 1051 |
| 2. | Cross-bred cows | 132 | 1130218 | 8562 | 37 | 234676 | 6342 | 126 | 1180368 | 9368 | 58 | 268366 | 4627 |
| 3. | Local buffaloes | 23 | 168187 | 7312 | 9 | 46965 | 5218 | - | - | - | - | - | - |
| 4. | Graded buffaloes | 19 | 272588 | 14346 | 7 | 72065 | 10295 | 2 | 16240 | 8124 | 2 | 10784 | 5392 |
| | All | 291 | 1703125 | 5852 | 114 | 410825 | 3603 | 201 | 1290121 | 6418 | 89 | 309629 | 3478 |

**Table 5.3 : Pattern of Investment per Animal in Dairy Farming (in Rs.)**

| Sl. No. | Particulars | Ganjam | | | | | Puri | | | | |
|---|---|---|---|---|---|---|---|---|---|---|---|
| | | LL | MF | SF | LF | Overall | LL | MF | SF | LF | Overall |
| 0 | 1 | 2 | 3 | 4 | 5 | 6 | 7 | 8 | 9 | 10 | 11 |
| **1.** | **Buffalo** | | | | | | | | | | |
| | Shed | 1522 | 2118 | 6322 | 8232 | 4318 | 1851 | 2167 | 8081 | 9342 | 5132 |
| | Equipments | 103 | 173 | 218 | 311 | 223 | 98 | 111 | 306 | 432 | 216 |
| | Animal | 5849 | 9361 | 12321 | 14823 | 11521 | 6287 | 7532 | 11821 | 16213 | 11826 |
| | Total | 7381 | 11652 | 18861 | 23366 | 12316 | 8236 | 9810 | 20208 | 25987 | 14374 |
| **2.** | **Cross Bred Cows** | | | | | | | | | | |
| | Shed | 2511 | 2836 | 3216 | 3391 | 2783 | 3161 | 2957 | 3418 | 3483 | 3154 |
| | Equipments | 141 | 182 | 191 | 203 | 189 | 162 | 224 | 197 | 212 | 203 |
| | Animal | 8628 | 9512 | 11313 | 11538 | 10158 | 9618 | 10320 | 12018 | 14815 | 11174 |
| | Total | 11280 | 12530 | 14720 | 15132 | 10391 | 12941 | 13501 | 15633 | 18510 | 13146 |

| **3. Non-descript Cows** | | | | | | | | | | |
|---|---|---|---|---|---|---|---|---|---|---|
| Shed | 331 | 428 | 456 | 521 | 407 | 218 | 467 | 521 | 549 | 421 |
| Equipments | 29 | 42 | 47 | 58 | 47 | 34 | 53 | 61 | 73 | 59 |
| Animal | 1263 | 1432 | 1895 | 1832 | 1643 | 1398 | 1473 | 1922 | 1941 | 1696 |
| Total | 1623 | 1902 | 2398 | 2411 | 2163 | 1650 | 1993 | 2504 | 2563 | 2184 |

reported for buffaloes followed by crossbred cows and non-descript cows. On the other hand, in Puri, the mean investment for buffaloes is found highest. Again the mean investment for each type of milch animal is highest incurred by large farmers, followed by small farmers, marginal farmers and landless agricultural labourers in both the districts under study.

## AVERAGE SIZE OF LIVESTOCK HOLDING

The income classwise average size of livestock holding is presented in Table 5.4 on the basis of annual household income, sample households are classified under three parts as bottom 33.33 per cent, middle 33.33 per cent and top 33.33 per cent. For all households the average possession of bovine animals is 3.60 whereas the corresponding figures for top 33 per cent of the households are 4.95 and bottom 33 per cent of the household it is 2.42 and for the middle 33 per cent it is 3.97. On the other hand, in Puri, the average size of livestock holding for the top 33%, middle 33 per cent and bottom 33 per cent are found at 3.12, 2.17, and 0.38 per cent respectively. The average bovine stock among all income categories among all households in Ganjam district is found higher than Puri district.

## MILK YIELD, FEED INTAKE AND HUMAN LABOUR PER MILCH ANIMAL

The average milk yield, feed intake and human labour per milch animal are shown in Table 5.5. The average milk yield per milch animal among the dairy households in Ganjam is found higher in comparison to non-dairy households. It is due to the better quantity and quality of fodder practices of the dairy households. Besides, dairy households maintain the milch animals for commercial point of view and consequently undertake timely care. Almost similar pattern is observed in Puri district also. It is found that the average milk yield in Puri is better than in Ganjam District. It is because of higher fodder and human labour arrangement made by the cattle owners in Puri district. From the table it is found that the average milk yield in Ganjam and Puri is found to be 4.37 and 4.69 per cent respectively.

**Table 5.4 : Average Size of the Livestock-holding of Sample Animals**

| Sl. No. | Types of Animals | Ganjam | | | | Puri | | | |
|---|---|---|---|---|---|---|---|---|---|
| | | Bottom 33% | Middle 33% | Top 33% | Overall | Bottom 33% | Middle 33% | Top 33% | Overall |
| 0 | 1 | 2 | 3 | 4 | 5 | 6 | 7 | 8 | 9 |
| 1. | Bullock | 1.34 | 2.13 | 2.03 | 1.72 | 0.81 | 0.65 | 0.79 | 0.75 |
| 2. | Non-descript | 0.87 | 1.29 | 1.92 | 1.32 | 0.67 | 0.89 | 0.63 | 0.78 |
| 3. | Cross-bred cow | 0.16 | 0.42 | 0.42 | 0.35 | 1.42 | 12.56 | 2.78 | 2.37 |
| 4. | Buffaloes | 0.05 | 0.13 | 0.58 | 0.21 | 0.02 | - | - | - |
| 5. | Goats | 3.45 | 1.24 | 0.45 | 1.47 | 0.01 | - | - | - |
| 6. | Sheep | .21 | 0.00 | 0.18 | 0.11 | 0.01 | - | - | - |
| All bovine animals | | 2.42 | 3.97 | 4.95 | 3.60 | 0.38 | 2.17 | 3.12 | 1.59 |

**Table 5.5: Average Daily Milk Yield, Feed Intake and Human Labour Per Milch Animal among the Sample Households**

| Sl. No. | Dairy | Ganjam | | | Puri | | |
|---|---|---|---|---|---|---|---|
| | | Non-HHs | All Dairy HHs | Dairy HHs | Non-HHs | All Dairy HHs | HHs |
| 0 | 1 | 2 | 3 | 4 | 5 | 6 | 7 |
| 1. | Average Milk Yield (litres) | 8.37 | 2.32 | 4.37 | 9.29 | 3.16 | 4.69 |
| 2. | Qty. of Green Fodder Fed (in kg) | 6.32 | 3.58 | 3.28 | 4.12 | 5.29 | 4.17 |
| 3. | Qty of Dry Fodder Fed (in kg) | 5.98 | 1.25 | 3.25 | 6.32 | 1.73 | 3.57 |
| 4. | Qty of concentrates | 4.78 | 1.5 | 2.14 | 3.13 | 0.51 | 1.84 |
| 5. | Human Labour Used (Minutes) | 125 | 82 | 103 | 142 | 102 | 116 |

## MILK MARKETING SYSTEM

The milk marketing system of the sample households is presented in Table 5.6. In the study area, three types of milk marketing systems prevail. Around 35 per cent of the dairy households supply their milk to primary milk producers cooperative, 38 per cent of the households supply their milk to vendor and the rest 37 per cent to the consumers in Ganjam district. In Puri district, the proportionate share of milk marketing is again found highest for cooperatives (41%) followed by direct selling 36 per cent and milk vendors (23%). The proportions of farmers directly sell to the consumer's account 37 per cent in Ganjam district and 36 in Puri district. It is reported that many a times the dairy farmers are discouraged by the cooperatives on false pleas of bad quality milk and the payment is not instantaneous. Similarly, middlemen offer lower price which is around 30 per cent less than the market price.

**Table 5.6: Distribution of Households as per Milk Marketing System**

| Sl. No. | Milk Marketing System | No. of HHs (Ganjam) | No. of HHs (Puri) |
|---|---|---|---|
| 1. | Cooperatives | 35 | 41 |
| 2. | Middlemen and Milk Vendors | 28 | 23 |
| 3. | Direct Selling by the Farmers | 37 | 36 |
| | Total | 100 | 100 |

## FEED AND FODDER PRODUCED AMONG SAMPLE HOUSEHOLDS

It is a well known fact that feed and fodder is the most important and costliest input for dairy cattle production. Feed is necessary not only for production but also for maintenance of the animals. In the present study, only nutrient species have been considered for our estimation of requirements of feed and fodder. To overcome the limitation of assessing the requirements for different nutrient species in different age groups the measurements are based on standard cattle unit. Assuming that on an average a cattle unit requires total of 10 kg. dry matter @ 3 kg concentrate, 5 kg dry fodder and 2 kg green fodder of dry matter basis.

### Green Fodder

There is no practise of growing green fodder crops in the sample area. Again, it is reported that he availability of pasture lands are not sufficient in one of the sample districts i.e. Puri. However, due to nearby forest lands common property resources (CPRs), green fodder are plentily available at Surada block. On an average, the non-descript cows in Ganjam district are able to graze 6 hours a day.

## Dry Fodder

Paddy straw is the most common dry fodder available for livestock feeding. For estimating dry fodder availability in the sample area, time series data on fodder produced in Orissa are examined.

When we consider about the processing possibilities of the agricultural products the agro-industrial potential becomes manifold. In Orissa paddy is a principal crop for many farmers. By weight measurement, paddy plants generally produce 50 per cent of straw, about 10.5 per cent husks, 3.5 per cent of rice kernels, and rest 36 per cent are paddy (Srivastav, 1989, Sab and Srivastav, 1985). Thus about 64 per cent of paddy plants cannot be directly consumed as human food but can be readily utilised for fodder.

An estimation of bovine fodder produced from paddy plants alone during various years is calculated in Table 5.7.

**Table 5.7 : Fodder produced from paddy Plants in Orissa**

| Sl. No. | Year | Straw ('000 mt) | Husk ('000 mt) | Bran ('000 mt) | Total ('000 mt) | Fodder/ Bovine Animal/Day (in kg) |
|---|---|---|---|---|---|---|
| 0 | 1 | 2 | 3 | 4 | 5 | 6 |
| 1. | 1970-71 | 4100 | 430.5 | 143.5 | 4674.0 | 1.01 |
| 2. | 1975-76 | 4532 | 475.9 | 158.6 | 5166.5 | 1.07 |
| 3. | 1980-81 | 4301 | 451.6 | 150.5 | 5903.1 | 0.96 |
| 4. | 1985-86 | 5226 | 548.7 | 182.9 | 5957.6 | 1.14 |
| 5. | 1991-92 | 6660 | 699.3 | 233.1 | 47592.4 | 1.40 |
| 6. | 1995-96 | 6226 | 563.7 | 217.9 | 709.6 | 1.20 |
| 7. | 2000-01 | 4613 | 484.4 | 161.5 | 5258.9 | 0.96 |
| 8. | 2001-02 | 7149 | 750.6 | 250.2 | 8149.8 | 1.49 |
| 9. | 2002-03 | 3244 | 340.6 | 113.5 | 3698.1 | 0.68 |

**Source:** Estimated from paddy production for various years in Orissa.

It is discernible that excluding other crops paddy alone could provide fodder to our bovine stock at the rate of 4670.0 thousand MT in 1970-71, 4903 thousand MT in 1980-81, 7592.4 Thousand MT in 1991-92 and 7097.6 thousand MT during 1995-96. Again per capita availability of fodder from paddy crops in Orissa to a cattle/buffalo is estimated 1.02 kg in 1970-71,0.96 kg in 1980-81, 1.40 kg in 1991-92 and 1.20 kg during 1995-96, and 0.68 kg. in 2002-03.

### Concentrates

In view of high labour cost to collect green fodder, the cross-bred cows are maintained by pur concentrates. It is estimated that around 35% of the feeding cost are incurred for purchasing concentrates.

### Feeding Practices

It is found that about 41 per cent of farmers keep their cows solely under stall feeding conditions per cent of the farmers are feeding adequate amount of green fodder to their animals in sample area and the green-fodder is more during rainy season. However, feeding of dry fodder is noticed among all households with green fodder and concentrates.

## ECONOMIC TRAITS OF CATTLE

The reproductive performance of the cattle has an important influence on the economic contribution from dairying. Hence, some selected parameters, which reflect upon the reproduction performance of cattle, are also studied. This has direct impact on the economic returns from the cattle and livelihood of the cattle owners.

### Age at First Calving

As per Table 5.8 the mean age at first calving (AFC) for all animals in Ganjam for all milch animals is found at 29.16 months, which are 33.25 in Puri district. However, disaggregated data of different types of milch animals in Ganjam suggests that the mean AFC of buffaloes is found highest (34.28 months) followed by crossbred cows (33.33 month) and non-descript cows (31.5 months). Similarly, in Puri district also the mean AFC is found to be highest for cross-bred cows (34.2%) followed by buffaloes (32.5%) and non-descript cows (31.5%).

The mean AFC for non-descript cows between dairying households of Puri and Ganjam is found significant at 5% level of significance (3.959) for other animals the mean AFC is not significant. However, for all animals there is a significant difference between AFC in Ganjam and Puri districts (4.302).

## Lactation Number

Lactation number of milch animals is described in term of mean lactation number. Table 5.9 show the mean lactation number of the milch animals as reported in the study area.

The distribution of milch animals according to the number of lactations indicates that the mean lactation length is generally 2.82 for all types of milch animals in Ganjam, which are 3.30 in Puri. The mean lactation length of cross-bred cows is 3.06 and for buffaloes and non-descript 2.68. Similarly, in Puri, the mean lactation length of cross-bred cows is found to be 3.55 followed by buffaloes 3(.5) and non-descript cows (2.87). The mean lactation length for all types of milch animals in Puri is found better than Ganjam. During our field survey it is reported that, the owners prefer to sell their milch animals after 2-3 lactations because of lowering of milk yield after this stage.

Except buffaloes there is no significance difference between mean lactation length of the milch animals in Ganjam and Puri. The mean lactation for buffaloes is significant because the t-value is found at 3.690 at 5 per cent level of significance.

## Lactation Length

Lactation length is an important indication to asses the milk yield of an animal over a long period. Presently, for

**Table 5.8 : Distribution of Milch Animals on the Basis of Age at First Calving**

| Sl. No. | Age at First Calving (in Months) | Ganjam | | | | Puri | | | |
|---|---|---|---|---|---|---|---|---|---|
| | | Non-Descript Cows | Cross Bred Cows | Buffaloes | All Animals | Non-Descript Cows | Cross Bred Cows | Buffaloes | All Animals |
| 0 | 1 | 2 | 3 | 4 | 5 | 6 | 7 | 8 | 9 |
| 1. | 20-25 | 21 | 8 | - | 29 | 9 | 6- | - | 15 |
| 2. | 25-30 | 31 | 23 | 3 | 57 | 18 | 18 | - | 36 |
| 3. | 30-35 | 29 | 42 | 29 | 100 | 27 | 38 | 2 | 67 |
| 4. | 35-40 | 21 | 57 | 2 | 80 | 16 | 54 | - | 70 |
| 5. | 40-45 | 15 | 2 | 8 | 25 | 3 | 10 | - | 13 |
| | Total | 117 | 132 | 42 | 291 | 73 | 126 | 2 | 201 |
| | Mean Age at First Calving | 31.5 | 33.33 | 34.28 | 29.14 | 31.54 | 34.2 | 32.5 | 33.25 |
| | T-stat 5% level of Significance | 3.959 | 0.509 | 1.622 | 4.302 | | | | |

**Table 5.9 : Lactation-wise Distribution of Milch Animals**

| | | Ganjam | | | | Puri | | | |
|---|---|---|---|---|---|---|---|---|---|
| Sl. No. | Number of Lactations | Non-Descript Cows | Cross Bred Cows | Buffaloes | All Animals | Non-Descript Cows | Cross Bred Cows | Buffaloes | All Animals |
| 0 | 1 | 2 | 3 | 4 | 5 | 6 | 7 | 8 | 9 |
| 1. | 1 | 17 | 9 | 7 | 33 | 11 | 7 | - | 18 |
| 2. | 2 | 42 | 26 | 11 | 79 | 8 | 15 | - | 23 |
| 3. | 3 | 39 | 58 | 13 | 110 | 35 | 31 | 1 | 67 |
| 4. | 4 | 8 | 26 | 11 | 45 | 17 | 47 | 1 | 65 |
| | 5 and above | 11 | 13 | - | 24 | 2 | 26 | - | 28 |
| | Total | 117 | 132 | 42 | 291 | 73 | 126 | 2 | 201 |
| | Mean Lactation Number. | 2.68 | 3.06 | 2.68 | 2.82 | 2.87 | 3.55 | 3.5 | 3.30 |
| | T-State at 5% Level of Significance | 1.255 | 0.140 | 3.690 | 1.271 | | | | |

examining the lactation length of the milch animals in the study areas, the mean lactation length is presented in Table 5.10.

In Ganjam, the mean lactation length for crossbred cows is 8.08 months followed by buffaloes (6.09) non-descript animals (4.76) the overall lactation length for all types of milch animals stands at 8.05. On the other hand, in Puri, the overall mean lactation length for all type of milch animals stands at 7.16 the lactation length of non-descript cows, cross-bred cows and buffaloes are 6.05, 7.80, and 7.0 respectively. The overall mean lactation length in Ganjam is found to be higher than Puri.

The mean lactation length of all type of milch animals is not found significant between Ganjam and Puri district at 5% level of significance.

### Milking Period

The milking period of all type of milch animals among the sample households is separately shown in Ganjam and Puri district in Table 5.11. It is revealed from the Table that the mean milking period for all type of animals is found at 182 .46 and 190.53 in Ganjam and Puri respectively. Milch animal-wise milking period is found highest for cross-bred cows (205.03 days) in Ganjam district followed by buffaloes (195.42 days) and non-descript cows (152.34 days). On the other hand, in Purl district, the mean milking period for buffaloes stands highest, which is 225.5 days. It is followed by cross-bred cows (215.4 days) and non-descript cows (146.5 days). It is found that the mean milking period for all type of milch animals stands higher in Puri district.

## DETERMINANTS OF DAIRYING

For analysing the determinants of dairying among the sample households, production function analysis was used as an analytical tool. Linear Cobb-Douglas and Semi-log types of production functions were used to express the relationship between milk output per animal and various factors influencing it.

### Table 5.10 : Lactation Length of Milch Animals

| Lactating (Length in Months) | Ganjam | | | | Puri | | | |
|---|---|---|---|---|---|---|---|---|
| | Non-Descript Cows | Cross Bred Cows | Buffaloes | Overall | Non-Descript Cows | Cross Bred Cows | Buffaloes | Overall |
| 1 | 2 | 3 | 4 | 5 | 6 | 7 | 8 | 9 |
| 1-3 | 21 | 18 | 2 | 41 | 5 | 2 | - | 7 |
| 3-5 | 39 | 28 | 4 | 71 | 17 | 13 | - | 30 |
| 5-7 | 51 | 33 | 29 | 113 | 27 | 22 | 1 | 50 |
| 7-9 | 3 | 57 | 4 | 63 | 19 | 47 | 1 | 67 |
| >9 | 3 | 27 | 3 | 33 | 5 | 42 | - | 47 |
| Total | 117 | 132 | 42 | 321 | 73 | 126 | 2 | 201 |
| Mean Lectation Length | 4.76 | 8.08 | 6.09 | 8.05 | 6.05 | 7.80 | 7.0 | 7.16 |
| T-stat at 5% Level of Significance | 1.141 | 1.294 | 1.596 | 1.668 | | | | |

**Table 5.11 : Distribution of Milch Animals according to the Milking Period**

| Sl. No. | Milking Period (No. of Days) | Ganjam | | | | Puri | | | |
|---|---|---|---|---|---|---|---|---|---|
| | | Cows | Cross-bred Cows | Buffaloes | All Milch Animals | Cows | Cross-Bred Cows | Buffaloes | All Milch Animals |
| 0 | 1 | 2 | 3 | 4 | 5 | 6 | 7 | 8 | 9 |
| 1. | 0-90 | 18 | 4 | 6 | 28 | 13 | 3 | - | 16 |
| 2. | 91-180 | 63 | 37 | 5 | 105 | 42 | 17 | - | 59 |
| 3. | 181-270 | 32 | 76 | 28 | 136 | 14 | 97 | 2 | 113 |
| 4. | 271-365 | 4 | 15 | 3 | 22 | 4 | 9 | - | 13 |
| | Total | 117 | 132 | 42 | 291 | 73 | 126 | 2 | 201 |
| Mean Milking Period (in Days) | | 152.34 | 205.03 | 195.42 | 182.46 | 146.50 | 215.48 | 225.5 | 190.53 |

The variables included are the production functions are as follows:

$Y = f(x_1, x_2 , x_3, x_4, x_5, x_6, x_7)$

where

$y$ =value of milk product per animal per day (Rs.).

$x_1$ =value of green fodder per animal per day.

$x_2$ =value of dry fodder per animal per day.

$x_3$ =value of concentrates fed per animal per day.

$x_4$ =Human labour cost per animal per day.

$x_5$ =Age of the animal (years).

$x_6$ =Order of lactation (number).

$x_7$ =Miscellaneous expenditure per animal per day.

However, before doing the analysis, zero order correlation matrices were worked out and the correlation co-efficient were examined for multi-colinearity. From zero-order correlation matrices of the variables, it was observed that age of the animal ($X_5$) and order of lactation ($X_6$) variable was found highly correlated in all the breeds of lactating animals. In order to overcome the problem of multi-collinearity age of the animal ($X_5$) was deleted and then regression analysis was done.

In order to capture the effect of different seasons on milk production, the dummy variables representing different seasons ($D_1$ and $D_2$) were incorporated in the production function to indicate the variation in milk production attributable to changes brought about by climatic factors.

The final production function selected was:

$Y= f(x_1, x_2, x_3, x_4, x_5, x_6, x_7, D_1, D_2)$

where

$D_1$ =1 for summer season.

=0 for other season.

$D_2$ =1 for rainy season.

=0 for other season.

The optimum allocation of resources was done under the constraint of available capital as given. The simplest method is to maximise the profit function using Lagrange multiplier with the constraint equation.

Now, let us suppose the production function as:

$Y = f(x_1, x_2, x_3)$

and capital constraint as:

$P_1x_1, P_2x_2, P_3x_3 = C$

where $P_1$, $P_2$ and $P_3$ are input prices and $x_1$, $x_2$, $x_3$ are levels of inputs used. 'c' is the finite amount of capital.

The profit equation is

$$\Pi = P_y Y - \sum_{i=1}^{3} P_i X_i + \lambda \left[ \sum_{i=1}^{3} P_i X_i - C \right]$$

where: λ is Lagrange multiplier. The term

$$\left[ \sum_{i=1}^{n} P_i X_i - C \right]$$

indicates the restraints that the total amount spent

$$\left[ \sum_{i=1}^{n} P_i X_i \right]$$

on the inputs cannot be greater than the amount of the capital C.

To determine the profit maximising amount of each input, we take the partial derivatives of profit equation with respect to each input λ and setting them equal to zero i.e.

$$\frac{\partial \pi}{\partial X_1} = \frac{\partial Y}{\partial X_1} - P_1 + \lambda P_1 = 0$$

$$\frac{\partial \pi}{\partial X_2} = \frac{\partial Y}{\partial X_2} - P_2 + \lambda P_2 = 0$$

$$\frac{\partial \pi}{\partial X_3} = \frac{\partial Y}{\partial X_3} - P_3 + \lambda P_3 = 0$$

$$\frac{\partial \pi}{\partial \lambda} = \sum_{i=1}^{3} p_i X_i - C = 0$$

These equations are solved for $x_i$s and λ to determine the magnitude of inputs which maximise profit under the restraint set out above.

## Constraints in Dairy Development

The important constraints as perceived by dairy households are high cost of commercial feed and low price for milk. Although there has been upward revision of milk prices recently, the increase in the price of milk is not commensurate with the increase in the feed prices. In fact, the ratio of fodder price and milk price are increasing over the years which itself is a big disincentive for the farmers to continue in dairy activity.

Employment and feed intake on the dairy group as compared to the non-dairy group obviously demonstrate the wholesome impact of the HCDP on these parameters in the study area.

The regression coefficients, standard errors and coefficients of multiple determinations of the milk production functions for summer, rainy and winter seasons for different breeds of cows and buffaloes on the dairy and non-dairy households are presented.

## Summer Season

the independent variables included in the regression equation explained 72 to 82 per cent of the variation in milk production being maximum non-descript cows and minimum in local buffaloes on the non-dairy households. Among the different inputs, the regression coefficients of green fodder and concentrates were positive and highly significant in all the equations fitted. The concentrate was the most important variable, which had significant and positive regression coefficient in all the equations. On the dairy households, the regression coefficient of concentrates was maximum in the case of non-descript cows (0.1506) and minimum in the case of crossbred cows (0.0932). While in the case of non-diary households, the regression coefficient of this input was maximum in the case of non-descript cows (0.1734) and minimum in the case of local buffaloes (0.1724). It shows that the concentrate was the most important factor affecting the milk production in all the breeds of cows and buffaloes both on the dairy and non-dairy households. The regression coefficient of green fodder on the dairy households was minimum for graded buffaloes (0.0813) and maximum for cross-bred cows (0.1 063), whereas in the case of non-beneficiaries, the regression coefficient of this input was minimum for non-descript cows (0.0888) and maximum for local buffaloes (0.0896), showing the corresponding percentage increase in value of milk due to one rupee increase in expenditure on green fodder. Though the regression coefficient of dry fodder was positive it was not statistically significant in all the regression equations fitted, except for cross-bred cows on the dairy households. The reason for non-significant regression coefficients of dry fodder can be described to the lack of variation in the quantity of dry fodder. The regression coefficient of labour was significant only in the case of graded buffaloes and order of lactation was significant in the case of local buffaloes only. The regression coefficient of stage of lactation was negative and statistically significant for all the equations on both the groups. This shows that with the advancement in the stage of lactation of the animal, its milk yield starts decreasing after a period of time. The regression coefficient of expenditure on miscellaneous items such as minor repairs of cattle shed and store, dairy equipments, electricity and water charges, health care expenses, etc., was significant and positive in the case of graded buffaloes and significantly negative in non-descript cows on the non-dairy group.

## Rainy Season

An examination of the coefficient of multiple determination indicates that the various factors influencing milk production included in the production functions explained about 62 to 91 per cent of the total variation in milk production in the case of dairy households whereas on the non-dairy group these variables explained about 74 to 80 per cent of the variation.

The green fodder, dry fodder and concentrates were the important inputs in influencing milk production having significant regression coefficients. The coefficient of green fodder was significant and positive for all the breeds of cows and buffaloes on both the dairy and non-dairy group except for non-descript cows on the non-dairy group. The regression coefficient of dry fodder was also significant in most of the cases except for graded and local buffaloes. The labour input exercised a significantly positive impact on milk production for cross-bred cows and graded buffaloes on the dairy households and for local buffaloes on the non-dairy group. The order of lactation had uniformly poor influence in explaining the variation in milk production. The stage of lactation showed negative and significant coefficient for all the breeds of animals except for non-descript cows on the dairy group.

The regression coefficient of miscellaneous expenditure was significant for cross-bred and non-descript cows on the dairy households. Miscellaneous expenditure had uniformly poor influence on the non-dairy households and graded buffaloes due to lack of variation in the variable itself and also due to the low degree of engagement.

### Winter Season

The regression coefficient of green fodder was significantly positive for all the breeds on the dairy and non-dairy households except for graded buffaloes, indicating thereby that milk production would register an increase in all breeds with an increase in green fodder at their mean levels. The dry fodder had a significantly positive impact on milk production only for non-descript cows and graded buffaloes on the dairy group. The regression coefficient of concentrates was highly significant and positive for all the breeds on both the groups except for non-descript cows on the dairy group. The stage of lactation, as expected, had significant and negative impact on milk production for all the breeds. The coefficient of labour was significant and positive only for non-descript cows on the dairy households and that of order of lactation was significant and negative for graded buffaloes.

### Overall

The effect of seasons could be examined by testing the estimates of parameters for different variables by applying suitable statistical test of significance. This entails the comparison of magnitude of each variable in different seasons. Another way to study the seasonal impact is to introduce a dummy variable for each season into pooled data for a year and testing the coefficients of dummy variables for statistical significance. The latter method is more simple and straightforward than the former. The green fodder, dry fodder and concentrates were again the important inputs in the milk production having significant regression coefficients. The regression coefficient of labour was positive and significant for all the breeds on the dairy households. The stage of lactation had a negative and significant impact on milk production on both the groups of households. The dummy variables for and rainy season had negative regression coefficients on both the dairy and non-dairy households, except for local buffaloes for which the dummy variable for summer season was not significant. It confirms that milk yield is higher in the winter season as compared to the summer and rainy seasons in all the breeds of animals on the dairy and non-dairy households, except for local buffaloes where there is no significant difference in milk yield in the summer and winter seasons. This clearly demonstrated that the winter season contributed significantly to milk yield as compared to the summer and rainy seasons on both the dairy and non-dairy households.

## NET INCOME PER MILCH ANIMAL

Non-descript cows, crossbred cows, and she-buffaloes are maintained as milch animals in the study area. The net income per milch animal is arrived at by deducting the operating expenses from the sale proceeds associated with the different type of milch animals. For the sake of convenience, net income per milch animal is expressed in terms of net-income per milch animal per day. For analysing net income per milch animal per day, the annual sale proceeds of all the dairy households are converted into sale proceeds per milch per day. Similarly, per milch operating expenses per day is obtained by converting the annual operating annual expenses of all the dairy households.

**Table 5.12 : Net Income Per Milch Animal Per Day**

| Sl. No. | Type of Milch Animals | Dairy Households in Ganjam | | Dairy Households in Puri | |
|---|---|---|---|---|---|
| | | Sale Proceeds Per Milch Animal Per day) | Operating Expenses (Per Milch Animal Per day) | Sale Proceeds Per Milch Animal Per day) | Operating Expenses (Per Milch Animal Per day) |
| 1. | **Non-Deascript Cows** | | | | |
| | Per Annum (Rs.) | 2263 | 1358 | 2341 | 1791 |
| | Per Day (Rs.) | 6.20 | 4.21 | 6.41 | 4.90 |
| 2. | **Cross-bred Cows** | | | | |
| | Per Annum (Rs.) | 17420 | 10746 | 18358 | 11644 |
| | Per Day (Rs.) | 47.72 | 29.44 | 50.29 | 31.90 |
| 3. | **Buffaloes** | | | | |
| | Per Annum (Rs.) | 14887 | 11247 | 12688 | 9346 |
| | Per day (Rs.) | 40.78 | 30.81 | 34.76 | 25.60 |

The annual operating expenses include the expenses incurred on fodder, operation and maintenance of shed, value of labour, veterinary expenses, interest paid on loans, and miscellaneous expenses such as purchase of tether and chains etc. In the operating expenses the depreciation value of milch animals has not been considered. Net income for all categories of milch animals is separately shown in Table 5.15 for the dairy households in Ganjam and Puri districts.

It is revealed from the above table that per day sale proceeds and operating expenses for non-descript cows are estimated at 6.20 and 4.21 respectively in Ganjam district. Thus, net-income per non-descript cows is found at Rs. 1.99. This figure is further lower in Puri district, where sale proceeds and operating expenses per milch animals are Rs. 6.41 and Rs. 4.90 respectively.

As against the sale proceeds and operating expenses, the net income per cross-bred cows is found at Rs. 18.28 and Rs. 18.39 in Ganjam and Puri respectively. For buffaloes the net income per day is calculated at Rs. 9.97 in Ganjam, which is Rs. 9.16 in Puri. It is observed that there is not much difference in the net income for all types of milch animals in the districts under study.

From the discussion made in this chapter, it follows that dairy sector contributes significantly to income and employment. It provides off-farm employment opportunities to agriculture labourers. Small farmers and large farmers have been benefited from dairying as a part of agro-diversification. It is found that during the milk-marketing process, dairy households are exploited by private milk vendors as well OMFED on flimsy grounds of poor quality milk.

# 6

# Socio-economic Status of the Sample Households

Socio-economic status of the sample households deserves sufficient attention in view of its intimate link with poverty, rural development and social change. Now-a-days social changes arising out of any development programme being visualised at many spheres. The present chapter analyses the socio-economic changes of households with sharp focus on changes in the socio-economic status due to dairy by comparing the socioeconomic status of dairy households with non-dairy households. The different indicators pertaining to the socio-economic status of both types of households are analysed on the basis of primary data obtained from the field survey conducted in Ganjam and Puri districts in Orissa (details shown in methodology in Chapter 1).

## AGE DISTRIBUTION OF SAMPLE HOUSEHOLDS

Age wise distribution of the members of the sample households is shown in Table 6.1. It is found that in Ganjam district majority of the sample population are in the age group between 0-14 years followed by 15-35, 36-55 and >55 years. Similar pattern is also noticed among both types of households. The sex ratio among dairy households and nondairy households is found at 901 and 738 respectively. The sex ratio among non-dairy households is much better than dairy households. In Puri district, the majority of the household members are in the age group of 36-56 years followed by 0-15 years, 15-35 years and above 50 years. Similar pattern is noticed among both types of households. The sex ratio among dairy and non-diary households in Puri district is found to be 956 and 862 respectively. From this analysis it is found that sex ratio among both type of households under study is better in Puri than in Ganjam. The overall sex ratio in Ganjam and Puri district is found to be 823 and 918 respectively.

## SOCIO-ECONOMIC CATEGORY OF THE SAMPLE HOUSEHOLDS

The classification of households on the basis of their social categories point out that majority of the households around 50 per cent is OBC households followed by other households. The proportionate share of se and ST households is found minimum which is only 6.5 per cent of the households studied in Ganjam district and only five per cent in Puri district.

In Ganjam district among the dairy households also, similar pattern is found out. As minimum as 57% of the dairy households are from OBC category followed by other category households. Only 13 per cent of the dairy households are BPL households as per the BPL cards issued by Government of Orissa. Similarly among the non-dairy households, 26 per cent of the households are under BPL category. In Puri district among the sample households 85% belong to the APL category and the rest are BPL households. Among dairy and non-dairy households the proportionate share of APL households accounts 89% and 80% respectively. Thus, on the basis of economic category, almost similar pattern is noticed for both the districts under study.

### Landholding Pattern

The pattern of landholding in the study area is shown in Table 6.3 it is revealed from the table that the bottom 33 per cent of the households own 0.8 hectares of land on an average;

**Table 6.1 : Age-wise and Sex-wise Distribution of the Population**

| Sl. No. | Age Group | Dairy Household | | | Non-Dairy Household | | | All Households | | |
|---|---|---|---|---|---|---|---|---|---|---|
| | | Male | Female | Total | Male | Female | Total | Male | Female | Total |
| | | | | | **Ganjam** | | | | | |
| 1. | 0-14 | 118 | 106 | 224 (37.24) | 107 | 88 | 195 (38.81) | 225 | 194 | 419 (37.08) |
| 2. | 15-35 | 88 | 82 | 170 (28.26) | 85 | 54 | 139 (27.05) | 173 | 136 | 309 (27.19) |
| 3. | 36-55 | 66 | 59 | 125 (20.75) | 52 | 52 | 104 (20.27) | 118 | 111 | 129 (20.09) |
| 4. | 56 above | 44 | 38 | 82 (13.64) | 51 | 24 | 75 (14.61) | 95 | 62 | 157 (14.56) |
| | Total | 316 | 285 | 601 (100.00) | 295 | 218 | 513 (100.00) | 611 | 503 | 111 (10.0) |

| | | | | | | | | | | |
|---|---|---|---|---|---|---|---|---|---|---|
| | | | | | **Puri** | | | | | |
| 1. | 0-14 | 109 | 98 | 207<br>(30.94) | 69 | 64 | 133<br>(31.74) | 178 | 162 | 340<br>(31.19) |
| 2. | 15-35 | 82 | 86 | 168<br>(25.11) | 67 | 56 | 123<br>(29.35) | 149 | 142 | 291<br>(26.11) |
| 3. | 36.55 | 117 | 91 | 208<br>(31.09) | 78 | 71 | 149<br>(35.56) | 195 | 162 | 357<br>(32.20) |
| 4. | 56<br>Above | 34 | 52 | 86<br>(12.85) | 11 | 3 | 14<br>(3.34) | 45 | 55 | 100<br>(9.1) |
| | Total | 342 | 327 | 669<br>(100.00) | 225 | 194 | 419<br>(100.0) | 567 | 521 | 128<br>(10.0) |

**Table 6.2 : Distribution of Sample Households on the Basis of Socio-economic Category**

| Sl. No. | Social Category | Dairy Households | | | Non-Dairy Households | | | All Households | | |
|---|---|---|---|---|---|---|---|---|---|---|
| | | APL | BPL | Total | APL | BPL | Total | APL | BPL | Total |
| | | | | | **Ganjam** | | | | | |
| 1. | SC | 1 | 3 | 4 | 0 | 9 | 9 | 1 | 12 | 13 |
| 3. | OBC | 52 | 8 | 60 | 38 | 8 | 46 | 89 | 16 | 106 |
| 4. | Others | 34 | 2 | 36 | 36 | 9 | 45 | 67 | 11 | 81 |
| | Total | 87 | 13 | 100 | 74 | 27 | 100 | 157 | 39 | 200 |
| | | | | | **Puri** | | | | | |
| 1. | SC | 3 | 2 | 5 | 2 | 2 | 4 | 5 | 4 | 9 |
| 3. | OBC | 38 | 5 | 53 | 44 | 9 | 53 | 92 | 14 | 106 |
| 4. | Others | 38 | 4 | 42 | 18 | 5 | 23 | 56 | 9 | 65 |
| | Total | 89 | 11 | 100 | 64 | 16 | 80 | 153 | 27 | 180 |

**Table 6.3 : Average Land-holding (in Acres) of the Sample Households**

| Land-holding | Bottom 33.33% | | Middle 33.33% | | Top 33.33% | | Overall | |
|---|---|---|---|---|---|---|---|---|
| | Ganjam | Puri | Ganjam | Puri | Ganjam | Puri | Ganjam | Puri |
| Irrigated | 0.9 | 0.51 | 0.11 | 0.72 | 0.75 | 4.7 | 0.30 | 2.70 |
| Owned | 0.03 | 0.05 | 0.11 | 1.34 | 0.75 | 3.13 | 0.26 | 2.27 |
| Leased in | 0.04 | 0.04 | 0.00 | 0.28 | 0.00 | 0.00 | 0.01 | 0.45 |
| Leased out | 0.02 | 0.03 | 0.00 | 0.1 | 0.01 | 2.51 | 0.04 | 2.34 |
| UnIrrigated | 00.7 | 0 .39 | 1.31 | 0.50 | 1.90 | 1.21 | 1.20 | 2.75 |
| All Types | 0.8 | 0.68 | 1.42 | 1.26 | 2.64 | 3.24 | 1.50 | 2.51 |

the middle 33 per cent of the households own 1.42 hectares of land and the top 33 per cent of the households own 2.64 hectares of land in Ganjam. The overall mean landholding of all the households in this district is 1.50 hectares. Similarly, in Puri district, the average landholding for top 3 per cent, middle 33 per cent and bottom 33 per cent of the sample households are 3.54, 1.26, and 0.68 hectares respectively. Except the top 33 per cent of the households, the average landholding in Ganjam is found better than Puri district.

## DISTRIBUTION OF RESPONDENTS ON THE BASIS OF LANDHOLDINGS

The distribution of respondent households on the basis of the size of landholding has been classified under 4 categories such as landless households, marginal farmers (up to 1 hectare of land), small farmers (1-2 hectare of land) and large farmers (more than two hectares of land). The proportionate share of landless labourers and marginal farmers stands at 30 per cent in Ganjam district. Big farmers account around 13 per cent among all the sample households. Big and small farmers jointly constitute around 71 per cent of the dairy households and 59 per cent among the non-dairy households. In Puri district, around 46 per cent of he dairy households are big and small farmers. It is inferred from the analysis that landless labourers are also reported in dairy activity. Due to the lack of on farm and off-farm employment opportunities in rural areas, most often landless people pursue dairying as a promising economic activity.

## WORK PARTICIPATION

The work participation of the sample households is analysed on the basis of main workers, marginal workers and non-workers. Main workers are those workers who have got 240 days work preceding to the year of survey, marginal workers are those workers who have employed for 180 days during the preceding year and non workers are those who have not got any type of employment opportunity during last year.

**Table 6.4 : Distribution of Sample Household on the Basis of the Size of Land-holding**

| Land-holding in acre | No. of Dairy Households | | No. of Non-Dairy | | All Households | |
|---|---|---|---|---|---|---|
| | Ganjam | Puri | Ganjam | Puri | Ganjam | Puri |
| Landless (No Land) | 18 | 10 | 8 | 8 | 26 (13.00) | 18 (10.0) |
| Marginal Farmer | 11 | 44 | 30 | 42 | 41 (20.50) | 86 (47.78) |
| Small Farmers (1-5) | 45 | 38 | 43 | 26 | 88 (44.00) | 64 (35.56) |
| Big Farmers | 26 >10 | 8 | 19 | 4 | 45 (22.50) | 12 (6.62) |
| Total | 100 | 100 | 100 | 80 | 200 (100.00) | 180 (100.00) |

As per the statement given in Table 6.5, it is revealed that in Ganjam district, around 50.00 per cent of the workers are main workers followed by marginal workers (35.55%) and non-workers (14.45%). Almost similar pattern is also noticed in Puri district. However, among the dairy households, the proportionate share of main workers and marginal workers are almost equal. The incidence of main workers is relatively higher among the non-dairy households. From this discussion it implies that around 50 per cent of the households engaged in dairying are not able to get sufficient employment opportunities in the existing scale of their respective dairying. There is further scope of increasing milk production even among the dairy households. Further, the non-workers can also be motivated towards dairying.

## PATTERN OF EMPLOYMENT

The pattern of employment of the sample population is analysed on the basis of 7-fold occupational structure as self employed farming, self employment non-farming, salary,

**Table 6.5 : Working Participation of the Sample Households**

| Sl. No. | Working Status | No. of Persons in Dairy HHs | | No. of Persons in Non-Dairy HHs | | All Households | |
|---|---|---|---|---|---|---|---|
| | | Ganjam | Puri | Ganjam | Puri | Ganjam | Puri |
| 1. | Main Workers | 122 (43.72) | 146 (50.87) | 134 (57.51) | 117 (56.79) | 256 (50.00) | 263 (53.34) |
| 2. | Marginal Workers | 121 (43.36) | 117 (40.76) | 61 (26.18) | 58 (28.15) | 182 (35.55) | 175 (35.49) |
| 3. | Non-Workers | 36 (12.90) | 24 (8.36) | 38 (16.30) | 31 (51.04) | 74 (14.45) | 55 (11.15) |
| | Total | 279 (100.00) | 287 (100.00) | 233 (100.00) | 206 (100.00) | 512 (100.00) | 493 (100.00) |

agricultural wages, non-agricultural wages, pensioners and other works. Other works such as collection of minor forest products (MFPs), processing of MFPs, petty business etc. are classified as other occupations.

In Ganjam district, highest proportion of people are engaged in self-employed farming (48.24%) followed by agriculture wages (13.28%), self-employed non-farming (7.42%). Among the dairy households, around 65 per cent of the persons are engaged in self-employed farming as against 45 per cent in the case of non-dairy households. The incidence of Agriculture wages and non-agriculture wages is also marginally noticed among dairy households. In Puri district also highest proportion of the dairy as well as non-diary households are found in self-employed farming.

## ANNUAL HOUSEHOLD INCOME

Annual household income is a major indicator to portray the socio-economic status. Presently for analysing the impact of dairying on household income, the mean income of the dairy households is compared with the corresponding figure of the non-dairy household and the difference between the two mean incomes is attributed to the marginal change in household income.

Table 6.7 reveals the mean income of all households is Rs. 46,500 and Rs. 48,000 in Ganjam and Puri respectively. On the other hand, the mean income of the dairy households and non-dairy households in Ganjam is Rs. 53,200 and Rs. 39,800 respectively. Thus, the marginal increases in the mean income of the dairy households in comparison to non-dairy households are to the extent of Rs. 13,400. Thus, due to dairying, the households have been able to increase their annual income to the extent of Rs. 13,400. Similarly, in Puri district the mean annual household income of the dairy and non-diary households is estimated at Rs. 54,800 and Rs. 39,500 respectively. The difference of mean income between dairy and non-dairy households is to the extent of Rs. 15,300, which is attributed to the marginal changes in animal households' income due to dairying. Thus, the influence of dairying on the

**Table 6.6 : Occupational Structure of the Sample Households**

| Sl. No. | Occupation | No. of Persons in Dairy Households | | No. of Persons in Non-Dairy Households | | All Households | |
|---|---|---|---|---|---|---|---|
| | | Ganjam | Puri | Ganjam | Puri | Ganjam | Puri |
| 1. | Self-employed Farming | 138 (49.46) | 142 (49.47) | 109 (46.78) | 89 (43.20) | 247 (48.24) | 231 (46.85) |
| [illegible] | [illegible] | [illegible] | [illegible] | [illegible] | [illegible] | [illegible] | [illegible] |
| [illegible] | [illegible] | [illegible] | [illegible] | [illegible] | [illegible] | [illegible] | [illegible] |
| [illegible] | [illegible] | [illegible] | [illegible] | [illegible] | [illegible] | [illegible] | [illegible] |
| [illegible] | [illegible] | [illegible] | [illegible] | [illegible] | [illegible] | [illegible] | [illegible] |
| [illegible] | [illegible] | [illegible] | [illegible] | [illegible] | [illegible] | [illegible] | [illegible] |
| [illegible] | [illegible] | [illegible] | [illegible] | [illegible] | [illegible] | [illegible] | [illegible] |
| | Total | 279 (100.00) | 287 (100.00) | 233 (100.00) | 206 (100.00) | 512 (100.00) | 493 (100.00) |

mean changes in household income is found better in Puri district. The overall mean income of all households in Ganjam district is lagging behind Puri district by an amount of Rs. 1,500.

**Table 6.7 : Annual Household Income of the Sample Households**

| Income (in Rs.) | No. of Dairy Households | | No. of Non-Dairy HHs | | All Households | |
|---|---|---|---|---|---|---|
| | Ganjam | Puri | Ganjam | Puri | Ganjam | Puri |
| <20,000 | 15 | 11 | 28 | 21 | 43 | 32 |
| 20000-40000 | 7 | 13 | 25 | 18 | 32 | 31 |
| 40000-60000 | 45 | 37 | 30 | 27 | 75 | 64 |
| 60000-80000 | 21 | 25 | 9 | 11 | 30 | 36 |
| 80000-100000 | 4 | 8 | 3 | 2 | 7 | 10 |
| >100000 | 8 | 6 | 5 | 1 | 13 | |
| Total | 100 | 100 | 100 | 80 | 200 | 180 |
| Mean Income | 53200 | 54800 | 39800 | 39500 | 46500 | 48000 |

## LITERACY STATUS

For analysing the literacy status of the sample population, data on educational qualification of all the members in the households were obtained. In the process, the children who have not attained the school going age i.e. less than 5 years were not considered. The classification of the sample population on the basis of their educational qualification is shown in Table 5.9.

It is found that among all sample households in Ganjam district majority of the members of sample households, 42 per cent have their educational qualification upto secondary level followed by primary (23.07%), higher secondary (20.17%) and above higher secondary (8.32%). The proportionate share of illiterate people is found lowest. Almost similar pattern is noticed among dairy and non-dairy households. Similarly in Puri district, the maximum proportion of the population as high as 42 per cent have completed secondary education followed by primary education (26.92%), higher secondary education (17.80%), no-education (8.97%) and above higher secondary education (4.70%). But slightly a different picture is noticed among the dairy households. Among the dairy households the proportionate share of illiterate people is only 3.5 per cent as against 60.11 per cent among the non-dairy households.

**Table 6.8 : Literacy Status of the Sample Population**

| Educational Status | No. of Dairy Households | | No. of Non-dairy Households | | All Households | |
|---|---|---|---|---|---|---|
| | Ganjam | Puri | Ganjam | Puri | Ganjam | Puri |
| Illiterate | 21<br>(4.50) | 14<br>(3.5) | 28<br>(8.56) | 49<br>(16.11) | 49<br>(6.17) | 63<br>(8.97) |
| Primary | 103<br>(22.10) | 78<br>(19.59) | 80<br>(24.46) | 111<br>(36.51) | 183<br>(23.07) | 189<br>(26.92) |
| Secondary | 179<br>(38.41) | 187<br>(46.98) | 156<br>(47.70) | 105<br>(34.53) | 335<br>(42.24) | 292<br>(41.59) |
| Higher Secondary | 114<br>(24.46) | 96<br>(24.12) | 46<br>(14.06) | 29<br>(9.53) | 160<br>(20.171 | 125<br>(17.80) |
| Higher Secondary & | 49<br>(10.51) | 23<br>(5.77) | 17<br>(5.19) | 10<br>(3.28 | 66<br>(8.32) | 33<br>(4.70) |
| Total | 466<br>(100.00) | 398<br>(100.00) | 327<br>(100.00) | 304<br>(100.00) | 793<br>(100.00) | 702<br>(100.00) |

## MEAN YEARS OF SCHOOLING

In recent years 'mean years of schooling' is being considered as a robust indicator for the sake of analysing human development performance of a particular region. The mean years of schooling in the study area is presented in Table 6.9.

The mean years of schooling among household members in Ganjam is calculated at 8.28 which are 8.56 among the dairy households and 7.82 among non-dairy households. Perhaps, due to increased income arising out of dairying, the access to education is better availed among the dairy households. In Puri district, the overall mean years of schooling are estimated at 7.33, which is 6.89 among the dairy households and 6.56 among the non-diary households.

**Table 6.9 : Years of Schooling**

| Years of Schooling | No. of Dairy Households | | No. of Non-Dairy Households | | All Households | |
|---|---|---|---|---|---|---|
| | Ganjam | Puri | Ganjam | Puri | Ganjam | Puri |
| 0 | 21 | 32 | 28 | 31 | 49 | 63 |
| 1 | 5 | 18 | 8 | 11 | 13 | 29 |
| 2 | 3 | 23 | 2 | 25 | 5 | 48 |
| 3 | 9 | 14 | 7 | 19 | 16 | 33 |
| 4 | 9 | 13 | 7 | 41 | 16 | 24 |
| 5 | 13 | 11 | 9 | 15 | 22 | 26 |
| 6 | 74 | 65 | 48 | 41 | 122 | 10 |
| 7 | 21 | 69 | 15 | 16 | 36 | 85 |
| 8 | 27 | 21 | 24 | 21 | 51 | 42 |
| 9 | 14 | 11 | 12 | 8 | 26 | 19 |
| 10 | 44 | 35 | 29 | 11 | 73 | 46 |
| 11 | 44 | 21 | 29 | 22 | 123 | 43 |
| 12 | 74 | 41 | 49 | 7 | 55 | 78 |
| 13 | 27 | 23 | 28 | 21 | 136 | 44 |
| 14 | 94 | 14 | 42 | 19 | 28 | 33 |
| 15 | 24 | 13 | 14 | 11 | 38 | 24 |
| Total | 466 | 424 | 327 | 319 | 793 | 742 |
| Mean years of Schooling | 8.56 | 6.89 | 7.82 | 6.56 | 8.28 | 7.36 |

## PHYSICAL ASSETS

The asset holding particulars of the sample households is ana analysed by examining a broad list of consumer durables possessed by the sample households. The incidence of all the assets is calculated per 100 households. The details of the asset holding particulars of dairy households as well as non-dairy households are separately shown in 6.10.

**Table 6.10: Asset Holding Particulars of the Sample Households**

| Assets | No. of Dairy House-holds Ganjam | No. of Non-Dairy HHs Puri | No. of Dairy House-holds Ganjam | No. of Non-Dairy HHs Puri |
|---|---|---|---|---|
| 1 | 2 | 3 | 4 | 5 |
| Radio | 0.07 | 0.10 | 0.053 | 0.04 |
| Fan | 0.35 | 0.41 | 0.131 | 0.16 |
| Torch | 0.09 | 0.22 | 0.053 | 0.10 |
| Lantern | 0.53 | 0.42 | 0.271 | 0.48 |
| Gas-Light | 0.01 | 0.04 | 0.003 | 0.02 |
| Water-Boiler | 0.79 | 0.81 | 0.363 | 0.39 |
| Baskets | 0.89 | 0.92 | 0.178 | 0.19 |
| Kerosene Stove | 0.21 | 0.35 | 0.112 | 0.16 |
| Gas Stove | 0.43 | 0.50 | 0.159 | 0.18 |
| Bicycle | 0.89 | 0.81 | 0.621 | 0.62 |
| Motor Cycle | 0.41 | 0.59 | 0.031 | 0.06 |
| Four Wheeler | 0.00 | 0.02 | 0.000 | 0.00 |
| Cot and Sofa Set | 0.13 | 0.22 | 0.008 | 0.02 |
| Steel Furniture | 0.89 | 0.98 | 0.157 | 0.25 |
| Watch/Clock/Timepiece | 0.98 | 0.99 | 0.521 | 0.52 |
| Camera | 0.05 | 0.07 | 0.003 | 0.03 |
| Television | 0.83 | 0.91 | 0.219 | 0.32 |
| CD Player | 0.01 | 0.09 | 0.001 | 0.02 |

*(contd.)*

| 1 | 2 | 3 | 4 | 5 |
|---|---|---|---|---|
| Washing Machine | 0.02 | 0.08 | 0.000 | 0.00 |
| Pressure Cooker | 0.51 | 0.64 | 0.019 | 0.09 |
| Mixer-Grinder | 0.41 | 0.58 | 0.012 | 0.02 |
| Electric Iron | 0.068 | 0.72 | 0.138 | .22 |
| Refrigerator | 0.04 | 0.05 | 0.012 | 0.01 |
| Wells Inside House | 0.49 | 0.59 | 0.291 | 0.32 |
| Electric Pump Set for Domestic Purpose | 0.05 | 0.55 | 0.008 | |

It is revealed from the Table that 83.7 per cent of dairy households are having television which is only 219 in non-dairy households in Ganjam district. As against 52.1 per cent own watches, only 9.8 per cent of non-dairy households own watches. Similarly, the incidence of motor cycle, pressure cooker, steel furniture, dug wells etc. among dairy households are mostly reported. On the basis of asset holding details, it is fair enough to say that dairy households command more entitlement than non-dairy households. Equally, Puri district marks the same trend.

## FINANCIAL ASSETS

The distribution of households on the basis of their financial assets is presented in Table 6.11. The possession of financial assets is shown separately for dairy and non-dairy households.

It is revealed that 48 per cent of the households have a Bank deposit, 29 per cent of households have post office deposits, 24 per cent of households have LIC policies, 15% households have some form of bonds/debentures and four per cent households have company shares/securities in Ganjam district. On other hand 16 per cent of the households have bank deposits and the 7% of the households have LIC policies in Puri district.

In comparison to non-dairy households, dairy household excel more in all type of deposits. Even bonds, debentures, shares/securities which are not found among non-dairy households, which are reported among dairy households in both the districts under the study.

In Ganjam, among dairy households, almost 32% of the households have bank account which is only 16% in the case of non-dairy households. Similarly, 21% dairy households own LIC polices which is only 30 for non dairy households. Similarly as against two per cent of households own postal deposits among non-dairy households, it is more than 13 times higher among non-dairy households. Similarly, in Puri district, 37 per cent of the dairy households have post-office deposit as against 21% among the nondairy households. In other financial aspects also dairy households are better equipped than the non-dairy households. From this analysis it follows that dairy households have significantly better financial assets than dairy households.

**Table 6.11 : Distribution of Households on the Basis of Financial Assets**

| Sl. No. | Type of Financial Asset | No. of Dairy Households | | No. of Non-Dairy Households | | All Households | |
|---|---|---|---|---|---|---|---|
| | | Ganjam | Puri | Ganjam | Puri | Ganjam | Puri |
| 1. | Post-Office Deposit | 27 (0.27) | 37 (0.37) | 2 (0.02) | - | 29 (0.29) | 39 (0.21) |
| 2. | Bank Deposit | 32 (0.32) | 26 (0.26) | 16 (0.16) | 4 (0.05) | 48 (0.48) | 30 (16.67) |
| 3. | LIC | 21 (0.21) | 12 (0.12) | 3 (0.03) | 1 (0.01) | 24 (0.24) | 13 (7.22) |
| 4. | Bonds/ Debenture | 15 (0.10 | 6 (0.06) | - - | - - | 15 (0.15) | 6 (3.33) |
| 5. | Share/ Security | 4 (0.40) | 1 (0.01) | - - | - - | 4 (0.04) | 1 (0.55) |
| | Sample Size | 100 | 100 | 100 | 80 | 200 | 180 |

**NB:** Figures in parentheses is percentage to the respective sample size.

## HOUSING

### Type of housing

The type of housing of the sample households is analysed in Table 6.13. The type of housing is explained by discussing different aspects of housing such as nature of housing, condition of housing, type of floor, walls, and roofs etc.

In Ganjam, it is found that 96.0 per cent of the households reside in their own houses and only four per cent of the households stay in rented accommodations. Around 40 per cent of the households are having pucca households followed by semi-*pucca* houses (36.5%) and the rest are *kachha* houses (24.0%). In Puri, 90 per cent of the sample households have their own accommodation.

For 67 per cent of the households in Ganjam the condition of housing is good. The living accommodation for another 21 % of the households is liveable. Only 11.5 per cent households live in badly damaged houses. The floor condition of 80 per cent of the households is made up of stone, brick, and cement Only 20 per cent of the households are having thatched and mud type of floors around 70 per cent of the households has *pucca* and semi-*pucca* type of houses.

Maximum proportion of the households in Ganjam are having brick/mud walls (33.0%) followed by brick/cement (31.0%), thatch, mud (24.5%), and wood (11.5%). Almost equal trend is observed in Puri district.

The roof structure of the majority of the households (36.7%) in Ganjam made up of asbestos followed by thatched roofs (26.0%) concrete/slabs (22.0%) and tiled roofs (16.0%) in Puri, thatched and tile roof jointly account around 67%.

Table 6.12 further indicates that the pucca and semi-*pucca* houses jointly constitute 88 per cent among the dairy households which is 75 per cent among the non-dairy households. Similarly 82 per cent of houses are good among dairy households as against 52 per cent among non-dairy households. With respect to stone/brick/cement type of floors, brick/cement walls/asbestos/concrete/ slabs type of roofs, the

**Table 6.12 : Distribution of Households on the Basis of Type of Housing**

| Sl. No. | Type of Housing | No. of Dairy Households | | No. of Dairy Non-Dairy Households | | All Households | |
|---|---|---|---|---|---|---|---|
| | | Ganjam | Puri | Ganjam | Puri | Ganjam | Puri |
| **1.** | **Living Accommodation** | | | | | | |
| | Own | 94 | 91 | 98 | 72 | 192 (96.0) | 163 |
| | Rental | 6 | 9 | 2 | 8 | 8 (4.0) | 17 |
| **2.** | **Nature of Housing** | | | | | | |
| | Kuchha | 12 | 21 | 36 | 31 | 48(24.0) | 52 |
| | Pucca | 56 | 42 | 23 | 28 | 70(39.5) | 70 |
| | Semi-Pucca | 32 | 37 | 41 | 2 | 73 (36.5) | 58 |
| **3.** | **Condition of Housing** | | | | | | |
| | Good | 82 | 74 | 52 | 33 | 134 (67.0) | 107 |
| | Liveable | 11 | 22 | 32 | 37 | 43 (21.5) | 59 |
| | Badly damaged | 7 | 4 | 16 | 10 | 23 (11.5) | 14 |
| **4.** | **Floor** | | | | | | |
| | Thatched | 12 | 25 | 28 | 39 | 40 (20.0) | 64 |
| | Mud/Stone/Cement | 21 | 42 | 11 | 26 | 32 (16.0) | 68 |
| | Brick/Cement | 67 | 33 | 61 | 25 | 128 (64.0) | 48 |

| | | | | | | |
|---|---|---|---|---|---|---|
| **5. Walls** | | | | | | |
| Thatched/Mud | 23 | 29 | 26 | 27 | 49 (24.5) | 56 |
| Wood | 9 | 8 | 14 | 13 | 23 (11.5) | 21 |
| Brick | 29 | 43 | 37 | 28 | 66 (33.0) | 71 |
| Mud Brick/Cement | 39 | 20 | 23 | 12 | 62 (31.0) | |
| **6. Roof** | | | | | | |
| Tile | 11 | 21 | 21 | 22 | 32 (16.0) | 43 |
| Thatched | 14 | 36 | 38 | 43 | 52 (24.0) | 79 |
| Asbestos | 43 | 22 | 29 | 8 | 72 (36.0) | 30 (???) |
| Concrete/Glass | 32 | 21 | 12 | 7 | 44 (22.0) | 28 (???) |

**Table 6.13 : Distribution of Households on the Basis of Quality of Housing**

| Sl. No. | Quality of Housing | No. of Dairy Households | | No. of Non-Dairy Households | | All Households | |
|---|---|---|---|---|---|---|---|
| | | Ganjam | Puri | Ganjam | Puri | Ganjam | Puri |
| 1. | **No. of Living Rooms** | | | | | | |
| | One Room | 8 | 4 | 11 | 5 | 19 (9.50) | 9 (5.0) |
| | Two Room | 23 | 27 | 62 | 64 | 85 (42.50) | 91 (50.55) |
| | 3-4 Rooms | 59 | 69 | 27 | 11 | 96 (48.00) | 80 (44.44) |
| 2. | **Separate Cow-shed** | | | | | | |
| | Yes | 100 | 98 | 46 | 51 | 146 (73.00) | 149 (82.77) |
| | No | 0 | 2 | 54 | 29 | 54 (27.00) | 31 (17.22) |
| 3. | **Kitchen** | | | | | | |
| | Yes | 84 | 91 | 67 | 53 | 151 (75.50) | 144 (80.00) |
| | No | 16 | 9 | 33 | 27 | 49 (24.50) | 36 (20.00) |
| 4. | **Chullah** | | | | | | |
| | Ordinary Chullah | 42 | 61 | 67 | 61 | 109 (54.50) | 122 (67.77) |
| | Improved Chullah | 23 | 19 | 19 | 3 | 42 (21.00) | 22 (12.22) |
| | Bio gas | 24 | 6 | 6 | - | 3015.00) | - |
| | LPG Stove | 11 | 14 | 8 | 16 | 19 (9.50) | 30 (16.66) |

| | | | | | | |
|---|---|---|---|---|---|---|
| 5. | **Drinking Water** | | | | | | |
| | Open Ponds | 5 | 3 | 11 | 6 | 16 (8.00) | 9 (5.0) |
| | Dry Well | 26 | 37 | 31 | 21 | 57 (28.50) | 58 (32.22) |
| | Steam/river | 2 | - | - | 48 | 2 (1.00) | - |
| | Tube Well | 56 | - | 58 | 5 | 114 (57.00) | 94 (52.22) |
| | Pump Water | 11 | 46 | - | 5 | 115.50) | 19-(10.55) |
| 6. | **Toilet Facility** | | | | | | |
| | Flush Latrine | 3 | 1 | - | - | 3 (1.50) | 1 (0.55) |
| | Septic Tank | 17 | 25 | 16 | 8 | 33 (16.50) | 31 (17.22) |
| | Pit-Latrine | 24 | 67 | 35 | 31 | 59 (29.50) | 88 (48.88) |
| | Open Space | 46 | 17 | 49 | 41 | 95 (47.50) | 58 (32.22) |

dairy households are marginally better off than the non-dairy households. In this background, the housing characteristics of dairy households are better than non-dairy households.

**Table 6.14 : Source-wise Indebtedness in Ganjam and Puri District (in Rs.)**

| Sl. No. | Sources of Borrowing | Ganjam | | Puri | |
|---|---|---|---|---|---|
| | | Dairying HHS | Non-Dairying HHS | Dairying HHS | Non-Dairying HHS |
| 1 | 2 | 3 | 4 | 5 | 6 |
| 1. | **Institutional Sources** | | | | |
| *I.* | *Commercial Banks* | | | | |
| A. | No. of Households | 8 | 12 | 14 | 16 |
| B. | Avg. amount borrowed | 12500 | 18600 | 22750 | 16300 |
| C. | Avg. amount repaid | 9850 | 14850 | 18350 | 10800 |
| D. | Avg. amount outstanding | 2650 | 3750 | 4400 | 5500 |
| E. | Rate of Interest (%) | 8.5 | 8.5 | 8.5 | 8.5 |
| *II.* | *Regional Rural Banks* | | | | |
| A. | No. of Households | 3 | 8 | 11 | 7 |
| B. | Avg. amount borrowed | 13100 | 14500 | 12200 | 13650 |
| C. | Avg. amount repaid | 12300 | 10200 | 11750 | 8300 |
| D. | Avg. amount outstanding | 800 | 4300 | 450 | 5350 |
| E. | Rate of Interest (%) | 8.5 | 8.5 | 8.5 | 8.5 |
| *III.* | *Cooperative Banks* | | | | |
| A. | No. of Households | 2 | 4 | 6 | 5 |
| B. | Avg. amount borrowed | 9750 | 8500 | 17350 | 16800 |
| C. | Avg. amount repaid | 9750 | 6800 | 14200 | 11460 |
| D. | Avg. amount outstanding | Nil | 1700 | 3150 | 5340 |
| E. | Rate of Interest (%) | 9.5 | 9.5 | 9.5 | 9.5 |
| **II.** | **Self Help Groups** | | | | |
| A. | No. of Households | 12 | 22 | 8 | 22 |
| B. | Avg. amount borrowed | 6823 | 5348 | 6845 | 3870 |
| C. | Avg. amount repaid | 5250 | 3223 | 5230 | 1950 |

*(contd.)*

| 1 2 | 3 | 4 | 5 | 6 |
|---|---|---|---|---|
| D. Avg. amount outstanding | 1573 | 2125 | 1615 | 1920 |
| E.Rate of Interest (%) | 24 | 24 | 24 | 24 |
| **III. Non-Institutional Sources** | | | | |
| *I. Friends and Relatives* | | | | |
| A.No. of Households | 14 | 19 | 12 | 18 |
| B.Avg. amount borrowed | 5700 | 6400 | 8690 | 9320 |
| C.Avg. amount repaid | 5250 | 5100 | 7560 | 7650 |
| D. Avg. amount outstanding | 450 | 1300 | 1130 | 1670 |
| E.Rate of Interest (%) | 20 | 24 | 18 | 22 |
| *II. Village Moneylenders* | | | | |
| A.No. of Households | 3 | 7 | 5 | 9 |
| B.Avg. amount borrowed | 2800 | 3700 | 6800 | 8950 |
| C.Avg. amount repaid | 2400 | 2850 | 5400 | 7150 |
| D. Avg. amount outstanding | 400 | 850 | 1400 | 1800 |
| E.Rate of Interest (%) | 36 | 48 | 48 | 60 |

## QUALITY OF HOUSING

The quality of housing of the sample households are examined in the light of number of living rooms, separate cow-shed non attached to the living accommodation, existence of kitchen, type of chullaha used by the household, type of drinking water, and access to toilet facilities.

Analysis of the surveyed data indicates that around 90 per cent of the sample households are having more than 2 living rooms inside their houses in both the districts. Around 73 per cent of the households have separate cowsheds, around 75 per cent of the households have separate kitchens in their houses, around 45 per cent of the households use non-traditional chullahas like bio-gas and LPG stoves; more than 60 per cent of the households have access to safe drinking water (tube-well water and tap water) and around 52 per cent of the households have access to latrine facility.

## INDEBTEDNESS

The pattern of indebtedness is analysed on the basis of the sources of borrowing, The different indicators like average amount of borrowing, mean repayment mean outstanding and the rate of interest are examined for assessing the pattern of indebtedness among the sample households. Landless and marginal farmers till now borrowing from village moneylenders, friends and relatives in order to meet medical expenditure, expenses relating to social functions, education expenditure of children in case of unforeseen events etc. at a higher rate of interest. But focus group discussion revealed that their dependence on village moneylenders declined sharply after the emergence and functioning of SHGs in both the districts under study. Some of the peculiar findings in Galliam dairying and non-dairying households is borrowing from village moneylender made to meet the expenses incurred on liquor and other intoxicants. During the post-liberalisation period, comparatively easy availability of loans, emergence of SHGs and private financing agencies forced village moneylenders to reduce the interest rate and liberalise the terms and condition of providing loans. But the role of village moneylenders is still felt necessary for rural community to procure loans without any delay and formality. The loan amount to be repaid to banks in non-dairying household is higher than the dairying households both in Ganjam and Puri. It is one of the points to analyse here that in case of non-dairying households, average amount borrowed per household is lower than the dairying households. Whereas the average amount of outstanding is higher. In Puri district, the average amount of loan borrowed by dairying households is higher then their counterparts in Ganjam district except as in case of Regional Rural Banks (RRBs). In the non-dairying households also the average amount borrowed from commercial banks and regional rural banks in Ganjam is higher than their counterparts in Puri district.

Quality of housing of the dairy households is marginally better on the ground that almost all households have separate cow shed which is only 46 per cent among the nondairy households. Separate kitchens inside the house are reported among 84 per cent of the households which is only 67 per cent among the non-dairy households. Non-traditional chullahas like improved chullahas, bio-gas and LPG stoves etc. are used by 38 per cent of the households. Around 11 per cent of the dairy households in Ganjam and 14 per cent 0 the dairy-households in Puri have access to tap water which is not found among the non-dairy households. The quality of housing of the dairy households is comparatively better than the non-dairy households.

To sum up, the impact of dairying on the socio-economic conditions is significant enough in terms of mean increase in the household income, quality of housing, possession of physical assets and financial assets, and quality improvement in the housing condition of dairy households.

# 7

# Impact of Dairying on Rural Development

As dairying is having vast potential to raise the income of the people in the primary sector, it has strong bearing to push rural development. In Orissa, the incidence of poverty is massively a rural phenomenon on the ground that around 67 per cent of poverty affected households of the State reside in rural areas (Hann and Dubey 2002). Again rural economy is mainly agrarian, where 64.73 per cent of the total workers derive their livelihood directly from agriculture (the Census 2001). Maximum concentration of rural poverty as high as 86.95 per cent is found among marginal farmers, small farmers and agricultural labourers. Thus rural development, typically aims at improving the socio-economic life of poverty ridden people residing in rural areas.

In the event of the 'Operation Flood' programme, so many farmers in Orissa have undertaken dairying on commercial lines. In this background, the present chapter examines the impact of dairying on rural development. This is calculated by comparing the consumption pattern of dairy households and non-dairy households. The difference in the consumption pattern between the two categories of households indicates the marginal changes arising due to dairy activity. Because rural poverty is a major factor hindering rural development, thus, the incidence of poverty is among both the type of households is separately calculated on the basis of Cost of Calories Function as suggested by planning function. The difference in the incidence of poverty of the two types of households suggests the impact of dairying on rural development. Besides, selected human development indicators for both types of households have also been studied separately. The marginal difference in these indicators points out the impact of dairying or human development. In a nutshell, the present chapter ventures at examining the impact of dairying on reducing rural poverty and improving human development which constitute the bedrock of the entire rural development programme. For examining human development arising due to dairying, few indicators already discussed in Chapter 6, have been re-incorporated in the present chapter.

For examining the consumption pattern the different indicators like per capita per day consumption of cereals, pulses, pattern of consumption of other food items and non-food items etc. have been studied. The details of the indicators examined in the present chapter are as follows:

## PER CAPITA PER DAY CONSUMPTION OF CEREALS

From the household weekly consumption data on cereals, per capita per day consumption of cereals (PCPDC) are calculated by considering the number of members in a family. The distribution of sample households on the basis of PCPDC is separately shown for dairy and non-dairy households in Table 7.1. The mean PCPDC of all households in Ganjam stands at 634.0 g as against the overall mean PCPCD 650.2 in Puri District. It is found that the mean PCPDC of dairy households is 649 g as against 610 g in Ganjam. On the other hand, the mean PCPDC for dairy and non-dairy households is found at 618.00 and 635.00 respectively. The mean PCPDC of cereals of dairy households is slightly higher than the non-dairy households in both the districts. In the previous chapter, it was found that the mean income of dairy households is much higher than the non-dairy households. However increased income is not reflected in the consumption pattern of cereals because the essential commodities are relatively income

**Table 7.1 : Per Capita Per Day Consumption of Cereals**

*(in grams)*

| Sl. No. | Per Capita Per day Consumption of Cereals | No. of Dairy Households | | No. of Non-Dairy Households | | All Households | |
|---|---|---|---|---|---|---|---|
| | | Ganjam | Puri | Ganjam | Puri | Ganjam | Puri |
| 1. | 0-200 | 5 | 3 | 13 | 8 | 18 | 11 |
| 2. | 200-400 | 14 | 15 | 9 | 7 | 23 | 22 |
| 3. | 400-600 | 25 | 23 | 20 | 17 | 45 | 40 |
| 4. | 600-800 | 26 | 25 | 28 | 24 | 54 | 49 |
| 5. | 800-1000 | 17 | 23 | 24 | 19 | 41 | 42 |
| 6. | >1000 | 13 | 11 | 6 | 5 | 19 | 16 |
| 7. | Total | 100 | 100 | 100 | 80 | 200 | 180 |
| | Mean PCPDC of Cereals | 650.00 | 666.00 | 618.00 | 635.00 | 634.00 | 652.22 |
| | | 649 | | 610 | | 629.5 | |

inelastic. Again Engel's law also holds good that even if income undergoes some positive changes, the consumption pattern of the essential commodities like cereals remains almost unchanged.

## PER CAPITA PER DAY CONSUMPTION OF PULSES

As per Table 7.2 PCPDC of pulses among dairy households stands at 660.00 grams as against 51.9 grams among non-dairy households. In Ganjam, the mean PCPDC of pulses of dairy households is 74.5 grams which is found lower at 57.5 grams among non-dairy households. Similarly, the mean PCPDC of pulses of among dairy households and nondairy households in Puri district is found to be at 60.0 and 41.8 respectively. From this table it is further evident that the mean PCPDC of dairy as well as non-dairy households in Ganjam is better than the corresponding categories of households in Puri district.

## CONSUMPTION PATTERN OF OTHER FOOD ITEMS

The consumption pattern of other food items such as meat, fish, egg, confectionary and other processed foods is presented in Table 7.3. In order to explain the consumption pattern of other food items, the mean monthly per capita consumption expenditure (MPCE) other food items is separately calculated for dairy and non-dairy households in both the districts under study. From the statement given in Table 7.3, it is revealed that the MPCE on meat, fish of dairy household are higher than the corresponding values of nondairy households by 122.83 per cent and 44.97 per cent respectively in Ganjam district. However, the consumption pattern of egg is slightly lower among dairy households. There has been 223.89 per cent increase in milk consumption among dairy households. It is reported that some of the dairy households have substituted milk for egg. There is negligible difference in the consumption of vegetable. However there is significant difference in the consumption pattern of fruits, confectionary processed foods and biscuits. These increased in the consumption pattern of other food items are attributed to higher income of the dairy households.

**Table 7.2 : Per Capita Per Day Consumption of Pulses (in grams)**

| Sl. No. | Per Capita Per day Consumption of Cereals | No. of Dairy Households | | No. of Non-Dairy Households | | All Households | |
|---|---|---|---|---|---|---|---|
| | | Ganjam | Puri | Ganjam | Puri | Ganjam | Puri |
| 1. | 0-50 | 32 | 51 | 52 | 56 | 84 | 107 |
| 2. | 50-100 | 42 | 34 | 34 | 22 | 76 | 56 |
| 3. | 100-150 | 21 | 9 | 11 | 1 | 32 | 10 |
| 4. | >150 | 5 | 6 | 3 | 1 | 8 | 7 |
| | Total | 100 | 100 | 100 | 80 | 200 | 180 |
| | Mean PCPDC of Pulses | 74.5 | 60.0 | 57.5 | 41.8 | 66.0 | 51.9 |

**Table 7.3 : Pattern of Consumption of Other Food Items**

| Sl. No. | Items of Consumption | MPCE among Dairy Households (Mean Value in Rs.) | | MPCE Non-Dairy Households (Mean Value in Rs.) | | % Deviation | |
|---|---|---|---|---|---|---|---|
| | | Ganjam | Puri | Ganjam | Puri | Ganjam | Puri |
| 1. | Meat | 56.51 | 46.31 | 25.36 | 21.35 | 122.83 | 116.90 |
| 2. | Fish | 26.24 | 28.64 | 18.10 | 25.28 | 44.97 | 13.29 |
| 3. | Egg | 18.28 | 6.43 | 19.26 | 9.36 | -5.08 | -31.30 |
| 4. | Milk/Milk Products | 72.39 | 88.36 | 22.35 | 41.74 | 223.89 | 116.69 |
| 5. | Vegetables | 81.93 | 67.78 | 79.85 | 38.52 | 2.60 | 75.96 |
| 6. | Fruits | 21.72 | 20.89 | 8.43 | 6.64 | 157.65 | 214.61 |
| 7. | Biscuits/Snacks | 16.21 | 14.78 | 12.47 | 19.10 | 29.99 | -22.62 |
| 8. | Confectionary | 27.19 | 18.62 | 7.32 | 11.56 | 271.44 | 61.07 |
| 9. | Processed Foods | 7.48 | 11.48 | 2.11 | 4.56 | 254.50 | 151 75 |

N.B.: $\% \text{ deviation} = \frac{\text{Main value of dairy household - mean value of non-dairy households}}{\text{Mean value of non-dairy households}} \times 100$

In Puri district, the mean MPCE on meat and fish among dairy households are higher to the extent of 116.90 and 13.29 respectively. The decrease in MPCE on egg of dairy household is to the extent 31.30 per cent. The consumption pattern for milk and milk products among diary households is found higher to the extent 31.30 per cent. Even the MPCE on milk and milk products of the dairy households is found higher than the dairy households in Ganjam district. Increased MPCE on vegetables, fruits, confectionaries, and processed foods, etc. are reported among dairy households. However, there is higher MPCE on biscuits and snacks among the non-dairy households.

## CONSUMPTION PATTERN OF NON-FOOD ITEMS

With a view to understand the impact of increased income (due to dairy) on non-food items, the consumption expenditure data on 13 selected items had been obtained from the sample households. The MPCE on all these non-food items is separately presented for dairy and non-dairy households in both the districts under study in Table 7.4.

From the statement furnished in Table 7.4, it is found that in Ganjam district, there has been more than 300% increase in MPCE of dairy households in the items like telephone, entertainment, travel, toiletry and cosmetics. Similarly, for the times like hotel/teas hop and footwear, etc. 200-300% increase in MPCE is reported among the dairy households. More than 100 per cent increase but less than 200 per cent increase is found in MPCE on clothing fuel, medical expenses and education expenses of the dairy households. Around 97 per cent increase in MPCE on newspapers, periodicals is observed among dairy households. There is not much difference in the use of intoxicants, *pan*, *beedi* and cigarettes etc. among both types of households,

Form this discussion it follows that due to increased income, the dairy households are able to spend more on entertainment, health/education and other luxurious consumption due to dairy activity, there has been eye-catching changes in the consumption pattern of rural households, which is a positive sign of rural development.

**Table 7.4 : Pattern of Consumption of Non-food Items**

| Sl. No. | Non-Food Items | MPCE Among Dairy Households (Mean Value in Rs.) | | MPCE Non-Dairy Households (Mean Value in Rs.) | | % Deviation | |
|---|---|---|---|---|---|---|---|
| | | Ganjam | Puri | Ganjam | Puri | Ganjam | Puri |
| 1. | Clothing | 322.52 | 316.48 | 111.42 | 140.08 | 189.46 | 125.71 |
| 2. | Footwear | 7.30 | 8.40 | 2.11 | 3.16 | 245.97 | 165.82 |
| 3. | Fuel/Electricity | 161.73 | 188.68 | 65.18 | 67.81 | 148.12 | 178.25 |
| 4. | Toiletry/Cosmetics | 22.13 | 27.34 | 5.48 | 8.47 | 303.83 | 222.79 |
| 5. | Intoxicants | 25.78 | 14.82 | 23.27 | 18.62 | 10.78 | -20.41 |
| 6. | Pan/Beedi/Cigarette | 31.63 | 28.53 | 30.87 | 31.54 | 2.46 | -9.54 |
| 7. | Newspapers and Periodicals | 5.19 | 8.60 | 2.63 | 3.08 | 97.33 | 179.22 |
| 8. | Medical Expenses | 42.51 | 62.58 | 20.49 | 24.96 | 187.46 | 150.72 |
| 9. | Education Expenses | 68.65 | 91.82 | 30.19 | 34.19 | 127.39 | 168.56 |
| 10. | Entertainment | 130.51 | 88.40 | 21.23 | 17.75 | 514.74 | 398.03 |
| 11. | Restaurant & Teashop | 42.12 | 21.61 | 12.09 | 11.48 | 248.38 | 88.24 |
| 12. | Travel | 132.37 | 148.56 | 23.91 | 57.92 | 453.61 | 163.93 |
| 13. | Telephone | 39.93 | 61.74 | 5.11 | 12.36 | 681.40 | 399.51 |

In Puri district, the highest increase is reported on entertainment and telephone among the dairy households. Increased MPCE to the extent of 200-300 per cent is found for the items like toiletry, and cosmetics. MPCE on the items such as intoxicants, *pan*, *beedi* and cigarettes is found to be declining among dairy households. Similarly, on education, there has been an appreciable change among the dairy households which is also better than Ganjam district. On the basis of analysis of MPCE on Non-food items it is revealed that in Puri district, due to diary activities, there has been increased access to telephone, education, newspapers, lower consumption of intoxicants etc. Again increased spending on entertainment, toiletry, and cosmetic indicate the urban bias of rural households. In this background, the impact of diary and rural development is encouraged which are found the study of dairy household in both the districts.

## INCIDENCE OF FOOD POVERTY

As eradiation of food-poverty happens to the primary focus of all rural development programmes, in this chapter an attempt has also been made to focus on the incidence of food-poverty among the sample households. For assessing the incidence of food poverty, the methodology prescribed in the Sixth Five-year Plan technical note is considered. Accordingly, the households below PCPDC of less than 2400 calories are identified as the households affected by food poverty.

To arrive at calorie equivalents of PCPDC of all food items, the calorific values related with different food items are considered as per the list prescribed by the Planning Commission. The calories class wise distribution of the sample households is presented in Table 7.5.

It is found that four per cent of the dairy households and 13 per cent of the non-dairy households in Ganjam are having PCPDC with less than 2400 calories. These households are identified as the households affected by food poverty. Similarly, in Puri district 2 per cent of the dairy households and around 9 per cent of the non-dairy households are affected by food poverty in both the districts. Among all sample households around 6.8 per cent of the households are said to be affected by food poverty. As per our analysis, there are 1.5 per cent of the dairy households and 5 per cent of the non-dairy households in both the districts under study are found with calories' shortfall or food poverty affected households. Thus, in comparison to non-dairy households there has been 70 per cent reduction in poverty among dairy households. In this background, due to dairying around 50 per cent of the food poverty-affected households have been able to escape from food poverty, which is positive impact of dairying on rural development.

## HUMAN DEVELOPMENT

In recent years promoting human development is increasingly visualised in the emerging rural development strategies. With a view to understand human development potentials in the study area, few selected indicators like enrolment ratio, drop out rate, access to latrine and access of safe drinking water are studied. The performance of the selected human development indicators among diary and non-dairy households is separately highlighted in Table 7.6.

It is found that among dairy households in Ganjam district, enrolment ratio has increased by 15 per cent and dropout rate is reduced by around 83 per cent. There has been increased access to latrine and safe drinking water by 34.66 per cent and 15.57 per cent respectively. Similarly, in Puri district enrolment ratio has increased by 12 per cent and drop out ratio is declined by 56.14 per cent. Marginal access to and safe drinking waters is reported to be around 41 per cent and 13.21 per cent respectively. Thus, it is viewed that dairying activity in rural areas are also influencing the key parameters associated with human development, which is a part of the rural development.

To conclude, due to dairying there has been marked improvement in the consumption pattern of cereals, pulses, and other food items including milk and milk products. Much

**Table 7.5 : Distribution of Households on the Basis of Calorie Class**

| Sl. No. | Calorie Class (in Kcal) | No. of Dairy Households | | No. of Non-Dairy Households | | All Households | |
|---|---|---|---|---|---|---|---|
| | | Ganjam | Puri | Ganjam | Puri | Ganjam | Puri |
| 1. | Up to 1500 | 1 | - | 5 | 3 | 6 | 3 |
| 2. | 1500-2000 | 1 | 2 | 3 | 2 | 4 | 4 |
| 3. | 2000-2400 | 2 | 2 | 5 | 2 | 7 | 2 |
| 4. | 2400-3000 | 14 | 22 | 28 | 20 | 42 | 42 |
| 5. | >3000 | 82 | 76 | 69 | 53 | 139 | 129 |
| 6. | Total | 100 | 100 | 100 | 80 | 200 | 180 |
| 7. | No. of Households Below 2400 K. Cal. | 4 | 2 | 13 | 7 | 17 | 9 |

**Table 7.6 : Pattern of Human Development**

| Sl. No. | Human Development Indicators (in %) | Dairy Households | | Non-Dairy Households | | % Deviation | |
|---|---|---|---|---|---|---|---|
| | | Ganjam | Puri | Ganjam | Puri | Ganjam | Puri |
| 1. | Enrolment Rate Ratio | 100 | 100 | 87 | 89 | 14.94 | 12.36 |
| 2 | Drop Out Rate | 2 | 3 | 12 | 7 | 83.35 | 57.14 |
| 3. | Access to Latrine | 54 | 83 | 51 | 59 | 34.66 | 40.68 |
| 4. | Access to Safe Water | 67 | 60 | 58 | 53 | 15.57 | 13.21 |

urbanisation is found in that there has been increased consumption expenditure on entertainment, toiletry and cosmetics, clothing and footwear etc. The impact of such trend is also manifested in the human development indicators like good conservancy, better sanitation, improved enrolment, reduced drop-out rates and access to safe drinking water.

# 8

# Summary and Conclusion

## SUMMARY OF FINDINGS

However in Puri district females are comparatively more disadvantageous than Ganjam on the ground the sex ratio in Puri district remain 968 as per 2001 which is 998 in Ganjam district. More than 80 per cent of the population reside in rural areas and the incidence of rural population in Puri is 86.42 per cent which is higher than the corresponding figure in Ganjam district. Population density in both the districts is higher than the state average it is found that total workers and marginal workers constitute around 65 per cent of the total population in Orissa which is 67.6 per cent in Ganjam district and 54.98 in Puri district. Incidence of marginal workers in Ganjam districts is also found higher than Puri district and the overall situation in Orissa. The teacher student ratio in primary schools stands at 0.105 and 0.106 respectively in Ganjam and Puri which is 0.018 in Orissa.

So far as literacy rate is concerned it is higher in Puri in comparison to Ganjam (60.77%) and the state figure i.e. overall literacy in Orissa.

Similarly, the socio-economic indicators, more specifically the human development indicators like prevalence of safe delivery, percentage of children completely immunised Infant

Mortality Rate (IMR), Mean years of schooling etc. are favourable in Puri district in comparison to Ganjam District and all Orissa picture for instance IMR in Ganjam district which is 107 is much higher than Puri District.

That cropping intensity and irrigation intensity both are higher in the district in comparison to Ganjam district. Even though, the net irrigated area in Ganjam district is more than double the net irrigated area in Puri district, but lower cropping intensity and irrigation intensity of the district indicates lower agriculture practise among the farmers.

It follows that, the agricultural practices in Puri district is better than Ganjam district.

Among the total cows, crossbred cows account 31.12 and 22.69 in Ganjam and Puri respectively. However, in absolute terms, the total numbers of crossbred cows in Puri are three times higher than the crossbred cows in Ganjam district. In Orissa, cows and buffaloes are only treated as milch animals and present policies are aimed at increasing the number of cross-bred cows. It is found that Ganjam and Puri jointly account around 16 per cent of the state milk production. Except egg production, the production of milk, meat and fish is higher in Puri district in comparison to Ganjam district.

The incidence of poverty in Ganjam and Puri district is 40.73 and 20.09 respectively. Thus with regard to the incidence of poverty, Ganjam district is having higher incidence of poverty which is twice the incidence of poverty in Puri district.

There are one cattle and buffalo farm, three veterinary poly clinics, 34 veterinary dispensaries, 242 first aid centres and one disease diagnostic centre in Ganjam district. On the other hand, in Puri district there are one liquid nitrogen plant, four veterinary poly clinics, 451 veterinary dispensaries and 248 veterinary first aid centres.

It is found that Ganjam and Puri jointly account 7.57 per cent of the geographical area, 11.6 of the forest area, 10.9 of the pasture area, and 14.4 per cent of the agricultural lands of the state. Further, it is found that permanent pasture is higher in Puri district in relation to Ganjam district.

The normal rainfall and normal rainy days in Ganjam and Puri district is less than the normal figures prevailing in the State

It is found that around 73 per cent of the households in Orissa have one-two dwelling rooms, which is found lower in Ganjam (60.28%) and Puri (69.10%) districts. However, households having more than three living rooms are found higher in both the districts under study.

Around 34 per cent of the married couples are not having independent sleeping rooms. The corresponding figure is around 46 per cent in Ganjam district and 37 per cent in Puri district.

Around 11 per cent of the households in Ganjam district use tap water for drinking purposes which is comparatively lower in Puri and overall pattern in Orissa.

Only 27 per cent of the households in Orissa depend on electricity as the source of lighting. The corresponding figures in Ganjam and Puri district are slightly better.

It is found that 30.94 per cent of the households are having access to bathroom, 37.51 per cent of the households have access to latrine and 38.5 per cent of the households have access to drainage in Ganjam district. On the other hand, the households having access to latrine (17.67%), access to bathroom (10.50%) and access to drainage (30.16%) in Puri district.

Around 50 per cent of the households in Ganjam district and 46 per cent of the households in Puri district use firewood for cooking purposes as against around 70 per cent of the households in Orissa.

It is found that around 24 per cent of the households in both the districts are availing banking services which are roughly same to the overall performance of the state.

The possession of other consumer durables like radio, bicycle, telephone, scooter, motor-cycle, car/jeep/van etc. is found higher in Puri district. Even the performance of Puri district is better than the overall picture in the state. In this background, it is inferred that the state of rural development is better in Puri district than in Ganjam district.

Data on food grain production, area under food grain production and yield rate suggests that over years food grains production has increased in both the districts. However, area under food grain production has reduced in both the districts. Though yield rate of food grains shows continuously increasing trend, but, yield rate of food grains in Ganjam is found better than Puri District.

It is evident that forest area constitutes 30.21 per cent of the geographical area in Orissa which is 24.81 per cent in Ganjam District and only 4.06 per cent in Puri District. Though dense forests and open forests in Ganjam district ,account around 20 times and 15 times of the dense and open forest areas of Puri respectively.

The bovine stock of the sample households which consists of bullock, non-descript cows, crossbred cows/calves, buffaloes/ calves, goats/and sheep. Out of 1114 animal stock in Ganjam district 881 (71.21 %) animals among the dairy households and 259 animals (21.71%) among the non-dairy households are found. Major proportion of the bovine stock of sample households in this district consist of bullocks (24.56%) followed by non-descript cows (15.61%) crossbred cows (5.08%), buffaloes (5.08%) goats (5.43%) and sheep (0.32%). On the other hand, crossbred cows constitute a major share among the animal stock of the sample households in Puri district and the proportionate share of crossbred cows in the animal stock is around 26 per cent followed by bullock and nondescript cows.

The mean bovine stock of the dairy households, in Ganjam district stands at 8.81 as against the mean bovine 2.59 among the non-dairy households. As against the mean stock of all animals at 5.77 among the dairy households in Puri district, the mean stock of animals among the non-dairy households is found at 1.42. Thus, the average stock of animals per dairy households as well as non-dairy households in Ganjam is higher than Puri district. However, the mean stock of crossbred cows is marginally higher in Puri district.

In Ganjam district the mean number of animals among dairy and non-dairy households is estimated to be 5.77 and 1.33 respectively. The mean number of animals among dairy households is found to be highest for small farmers which are 8.1 followed by large farmers (7.9), marginal farmers (4.02) and landless households (2.6). The mean livestock households among the non-dairy households consisting of large farmers, small farmers, marginal farmers, and landless labourers are found to be 4.25, 1.92,0.88 and 0.37 respectively. Similarly, in Puri District the number of animals per dairy households is found at 9.0, which are 2.6 among non-dairy households. The mean number of animals among LFs, SFs, MFs, and LLs is 10.3, 9.0, 11.4 and 5.7 respectively among dairy households. The corresponding figures 3.9, 3.0, 1.2, 2.6 are found for LFs, SFs, MFs, and LLs respectively among the non-dairy households.

It is inferred that the average number of animals in Puri district is found higher among both the categories of households. Among dairy households the mean holding animal is found highest among small farmers followed by large farmers and others in Ganjam district. On the other hand, marginal farmers dominate so far as livestock possession is concerned.

Among the sample households in Ganjam district, there are 291 milch animals and 114 young stocks. The total value of all the milch animals and young stock are calculated at Rs. 21,13,950. The value per milch animal and young stock are calculated at Rs. 5852 and Rs. 3603 respectively. Similarly, there are 201 milch animals among the sample households in Puri District. The total value, average value per milch animals and the average value for young stock are found at Rs. 12,90,121, Rs. 6,418 and Rs. 3,478 respectively. The mean value of milch animals in Ganjam and Puri district are found at Rs. 5,852 and Rs. 6,418 respectively. Similarly, the mean value of young stock is estimated at Rs. 3,603 and Rs. 3,478 in Ganjam and Puri respectively. It is observed that the mean value of milch animals in Puri stand higher in comparison to Ganjam. On the other hand the mean value of young stock in Ganjam district is found higher.

The mean investment being influenced by various coasts like sheds, equipments, and animals remain different for different category of farmers. The overall mean investment in Ganjam district is highest reported for buffaloes followed by crossbred cows and non-descript cows. On the other hand, in Puri, the mean investment for buffaloes is found highest. Again the mean investment for each type of milch animal is highest incurred by large farmers, followed by small farmers, marginal farmers and landless agricultural labourers in both the districts under study.

For all households the average possession of bovine animals is 3.60 whereas the corresponding figures for top 33 per cent of the households are 4.95 and bottom 33 per cent of the households it is 2.42 and for the middle 33 per cent it is 3.97. On the other hand, in Puri, the average size of livestock holding for the top 33 per cent, middle 33 per cent and bottom 33 per cent are found at 3.12, 2.17, and 0.38 per cent respectively. The average bovine stock among all income categories among all households in Ganjam district is found higher than Puri district.

The average milk yield per milch animal among the dairy households in Ganjam is found higher in comparison to non-dairy households. It is due to the better quantity and quality of fodder practices of the dairy households. Besides, dairy households maintain the milch animals for commercial point of view and consequently undertake timely care. Almost similar pattern is observed in Puri district also. It is found that the average milk yield in Puri is better than in Ganjam District. It is because of higher fodder and human labour arrangement made by the cattle owners in Puri district.

Availability of fodder from paddy crops in Orissa to a cattle/buffalo is estimated 1.02 kg in 1970-71,0.96 kg in 1980-81, 1.40 kg in 1991-92 and 1.20 kg during 1995-96, and 0.68 kg. in 2002-03.

Around 35 per cent of the dairy households supply their milk to primary milk producers cooperative, 38 per cent of the households supply their milk to vendor and the rest 37 per cent to the consumers in Ganjam district. In Puri district, the proportionate share of milk marketing is again found highest for cooperatives (41%) followed by direct selling 36% and milk vendors (23%). The proportion of farmers directly sells to the consumer's account 37 per cent in Ganjam district and 36 in Puri district. It is reported that many a times the dairy farmers are discouraged by the cooperatives on false pleas of bad quality milk and the payment is not instantaneous. Similarly, middlemen offer lower price which is around 30 per cent less than the market price.

Due to nearby forest lands common property resources (CPRs), green fodder are plentily available at Surada block. On an average, the non-descript cows in Ganjam district are able to graze six hours a day.

About 41 per cent of farmers keep their cows solely under stall feeding conditions and 32 per cent of the farmers are feeding adequate amount of green fodder to their animals in sample area and the use of green fodder is more during rainy season. However, feeding of dry fodder is noticed among all households along with green fodder and concentrates.

The mean age at first calving (AFC) for all animals in Ganjam for all milch animals is found at 29.16 months, which are 33.25 in Puri district. However, disaggregated data of different types of milch animals in Ganjam suggests that the mean AFC of buffaloes is found highest (34.28 months) followed by crossbred cows (33.33 month) and non-descript cows (31.5 months). Similarly, in Puri district also the mean AFC is found to be highest for cross-bred cows (34.2%) followed by buffaloes (32.5%) and non-descript cows (31.5%).

The mean AFC for non-descript cows between dairying households of Puri and Ganjam is found significant at 5 per cent level of significance (3.959) for other animals the mean APC is not significant. However, for all animals there is a significant difference between AFC in Ganjam and Puri districts (4.302).

The distribution of milch animals according to the number of lactations indicates that the mean lactation length is generally 2.82 for all types of milch animals in Ganjam, which are 3.30 in Puri. The mean lactation length of cross-bred cows is 3.06 and for buffaloes and non-descript 2.68. Similarly, in Puri, the mean lactation length of cross-bred cows is found to be 3.55 followed by buffaloes (3.5) and non-descript cows (2.87). The mean lactation length for all types of milch animals in Puri is found better than Ganjam. During our field survey it is reported that, the owners prefer to sell their milch animals after 2-3 lactations because of lowering of milk yield after this stage.

Except buffaloes there is no significance difference between mean lactation length of the milch animals in Ganjam and Puri. The mean lactation length for buffaloes is significant because the t-value is found at 3.690 at five per cent level of significance.

In Ganjam, the mean lactation length for crossbred cows is 8.08 months followed by buffaloes (6.09) non-descript animals (4.76). The overall lactation length for all types of milch animals stands at 8.05. On the other hand, in Puri, the overall mean lactation length for all type of milch animals stands at 7.16 the lactation length of non-descript cows, cross-bred cows and buffaloes are 6.05, 7.80, and 7.0 respectively. The overall mean lactation length in Ganjam is found to be higher than Puri.

The mean milking period for all type of animals is found at 182.46 and 190.53 in Ganjam and Puri respectively. Milch animal-wise milking period is found highest for cross-bred cows (205.03 days) in Ganjam district followed by buffaloes (195.42 days) and non-descript cows (152.34 days). On the other hand, in Puri district, the mean milking period for buffaloes stands highest, which is 225.5 days. It is followed by cross-bred cows (215.4 days) and non-descript cows (146.5 days). It is found that the mean milking period for all type of milch animals stands higher in Puri district.

Employment and feed intake on the dairy group as compared to the non-dairy group obviously demonstrate the wholesome impact of the HCDP on these parameters in the study area.

The independent variables included in the regression equation explained 72 to 82 per cent of the variation in milk production being maximum non-descript cows and minimum in local buffaloes on the non-dairy households. Among the different inputs, the regression coefficients of green fodder and concentrates were positive and highly significant in all the equations fitted. The concentrate was the most important variable which had significant and positive regression coefficient in all the equations. On the dairy households the regression coefficient of concentrates was maximum in the case of nondescript cows (0.1506) and minimum in the case of cross-bred cows (0.0932) while in the case of non-beneficiaries the regression coefficient of this input was maximum in the case of non-descript cows (0.1734) and minimum in the case of local buffaloes (0.1724). It shows that the concentrate was the most important factor affecting the milk production in all the breeds of cows and buffaloes both on the dairy and non-dairy households.

The regression coefficient of green fodder on the dairy households was minimum for graded buffaloes (0.0813) and maximum for cross-bred cows (0.1063), whereas in the case of non-beneficiaries, the regression coefficient of this input was minimum for nondescript cows (0.0888) and maximum for local buffaloes (0.0896), showing the corresponding percentage increase in value of milk due to one rupee increase in expenditure on green fodder. Though the regression coefficient of dry fodder was positive it was not statistically significant in all the regression equations fitted, except for crossbred cows on the dairy households. The reason for non-significant regression coefficients of dry fodder can be described to the lack of variation in the quantity of dry fodder.

The regression coefficient of labour was significant only in the case of graded buffaloes and order of lactation was significant in the case of local buffaloes only. The regression coefficient of stage of lactation was negative and statistically significant for all the equations on both the groups.

The various factors influencing milk production included in the production functions explained about 62 to 91 per cent of the total variation in milk production in the case of dairy households whereas on the non-dairy group these variables explained about 74 to 80 per cent of the variation.

Green fodder, dry fodder and concentrates were the important inputs in influencing milk production having significant regression coefficients. The coefficient of green fodder was significant and positive for all the breeds of cows and buffaloes on both the dairy and non-dairy groups except for non-descript cows on the non-dairy group.

The regression coefficient of miscellaneous expenditure was significant for crossbred and non-descript cows on the dairy households. Miscellaneous expenditure had uniformly poor influence on the non-dairy households and graded buffaloes due to lack of variation in the variable itself and also due to the low degree of engagement.

The regression coefficient of green fodder was significantly positive for all the breeds on the dairy and non-dairy households except for graded buffaloes, indicating thereby that milk production would register an increase in all breeds with an increase in green fodder at their mean levels. The dry fodder had a significantly positive impact on milk production only for non-descript cows and graded buffaloes on the dairy group.

Per day sale proceeds and operating expenses for non-descript cows are estimated at 6.20 and 4.21 respectively in Ganjam district. Thus, net-income per non-descript cows is found at Rs. 1.99. This figure is further lower in Puri district, where sale proceeds and operating expenses per milch animals are Rs. 6.41 and Rs. 4.90 respectively.

As against the sale proceeds and operating expenses, the net income per cross-bred cows is found at Rs. 18.28 and Rs. 18.39 in Ganjam and Puri respectively. For buffaloes the net income per day is calculated at Rs. 9.97 in Ganjam, which is Rs. 9.16 in Puri. It is observed that there is not much difference in the net income for all types of milch animals in the districts under study.

It is found that in Ganjam district majority of the sample population are in the age group between 0-14 years followed by 15-35, 36-55 and >55 years. Similar pattern is also noticed among both types of households. The sex ratio among dairy households and non-dairy households is found at 901 and 738 respectively. The sex ratio among non-dairy households is much better than dairy households. In Puri district, the majority of the household members are in the age group of 36-56 years followed by 0-15 years, 15-35 years and above 50 years. Similar pattern is noticed among both types of households. The sex ratio among dairy and non-diary households in Puri district is found to be 956 and 862 respectively. From this analysis it is found that sex ratio among both type of households under study is better in Puri than in Ganjam. The overall sex ratio in Ganjam and Puri district is found to be 823 and 918 respectively.

The classification of households on the basis of their social categories point out that majority of the households around 50 per cent is OBC households followed by other households. The proportionate share of SC and ST households is found minimum which is only 6.5 per cent of the households studied in Ganjam district and only five per cent in Puri district.

In Ganjam district among the dairy households also, similar pattern is found out. As minimum as 57 per cent of the dairy households are from OBC category followed by other category households. Only 13 per cent of the dairy households are BPL households as per the BPL cards issued by Government of Orissa. Similarly among the non-dairy households, 26 per cent of the households are under BPL category. In Puri district among the sample households 85 per cent belong to the APL category and the rest are BPL households. Among dairy and non-dairy households the proportionate share of APL households accounts 89 per cent and 80 per cent respectively.

The bottom 33 per cent of the households own 0.8 hectares of land on an average; the middle 33 per cent of the households own 1.42 hectares of land and the top 33 per cent of the households own 2.64 hectares of land in Ganjam. The overall mean landholding of all the households in this district is 1.50 hectares. Similarly, in Puri district, the average land-holding for top 3 per cent, middle 33 per cent and bottom 33 per cent of the sample households are 3.54, 1.26, and 0.68 hectares respectively. Except the top 33 per cent of the households, the average landholding in Ganjam is found better than Puri district.

The proportionate share of landless labourers and marginal farmers stands at 30.00 per cent in Ganjam district. Big farmers account around 13 per cent among all the sample households. Big and small farmers jointly constitute around 71 per cent of the dairy households and 59 per cent among the non-dairy households. In Puri district, around 46 per cent of he dairy households are big and small farmers. It is inferred from the analysis that landless labourers are also reported in dairy activity. Due to the lack of on-farm and off-farm employment opportunities in rural areas, most often landless people pursue dairying as a promising economic activity.

It is revealed that in Ganjam district, around 50.00 per cent of the workers are main workers followed by marginal workers (35.55%) and non-workers (14.45%). Almost similar pattern is also noticed in Puri district. However, among the dairy households, the proportionate share of main workers and marginal workers are almost equal. The incidence of main workers is relatively higher among the non-dairy households. From this discussion it implies that around 50 per cent of the households engaged in dairying are not able to get sufficient employment opportunities in the existing scale of their respective dairying. There is further scope of increasing milk production even among the dairy households. Further, the non-workers can also be motivated towards dairying.

In Ganjam district, highest proportion of people are engaged in self-employed farming (48.24%) followed by agriculture wages (13.28%), self-employed non-farming (7.42%). Among the dairy households around 65% per cent of the persons are engaged in self-employed farming as against 45 per cent in the case of non-dairy households. The incidence of agriculture wages and non-agriculture wages is also marginally noticed among dairy households. In Puri district also highest proportion of the dairy as well as non-diary households are found in self-employed farming.

The mean income of the dairy households and non-dairy households in Ganjam is Rs. 53,200 and Rs. 39,800 respectively. Thus, the marginal increases in the mean income of the dairy households in comparison to non-dairy households are to the extent of Rs. 13,400. Thus, due to dairying, the households have been able to increase their annual income to the extent of Rs. 13,400. Similarly, in Puri district the mean annual household income of the dairy and non-diary households is estimated at Rs. 54,800 and Rs. 39,500 respectively. The difference of mean income between dairy and non-dairy households is to the extent of Rs. 15,300, which is attributed to the marginal changes in annual households' income due to dairying. Thus, the influence of dairying on the mean changes in household income is found better in Puri district. The overall mean income of all households in Ganjam district is lagging behind Puri district by an amount of Rs. 1,500.

Among all sample households in Ganjam district majority of the members of sample households, 42 per cent have their educational qualification upto secondary level followed by primary (23.077), higher secondary (20.17%) and above higher secondary (8.32). The proportionate share of illiterate people is found lowest.

The mean yeas of schooling among household members in Ganjam are calculated at 8.28 which are 8.56 among the dairy households and 7.82 among non-dairy households. Perhaps, due to increased income arising out of dairying, the access to education is better availed among the dairy households. In Puri district, the overall mean years of schooling are estimated at 7.33, which is 6.89 among the dairy households and 6.56 among the non-diary households.

It is revealed that 83.7 per cent of dairy households are having television which is only 219 in non-dairy households in Ganjam district. As against 52.1 per cent own watches, only 9.8 per cent of non-dairy households own watches. Similarly, the incidence of motor cycle, pressure cooker, steel furniture, dug wells etc. among dairy households are mostly reported. On the basis of asset holding details, it is fair enough to say that dairy households command more entitlement than non-dairy households. Equally Puri district marks the same trend.

It is revealed that 48 per cent of the households have a Bank deposit, 29 per cent of households have post office deposits, 24 per cent of households have LIC policies, 15 per cent households have some form of bonds/debentures and 4 per cent households have company shares/securities in Ganjam district. On other hand 16 per cent of the households have bank deposits and the 7 per cent of the households have LIC policies in Puri district.

In comparison to non-dairy households, dairy household excel more in all type of deposits. Even bonds, debentures, shares/securities which are not found among non-dairy households, which are reported among dairy households in both the districts under the study.

In Ganjam, among dairy households, almost 32 per cent of the households have bank account which is only 16 per cent in the case of non-dairy households. Similarly, 21 per cent dairy households own LIC polices which are only 30 for non dairy households. Similarly as against two per cent of households own postal deposits among non-dairy households, it is more than 13 times higher among non-dairy households. Similarly, in Puri district, 37 per cent of the dairy households have post-office deposit as against 21 per cent among the non-dairy households. In other financial aspects also dairy households are better equipped than the non-dairy households. From this analysis it follows that dairy households have significantly better financial assets than dairy households.

The mean income o^ the dairy households and non-dairy households in Ganjam is Rs. 53,200 and Rs. 39,800 respectively. Thus, the marginal increases in the mean income of the dairy households in comparison to non-dairy households are to the extent of Rs. 13,400. Thus, due to dairying, the households have been able to increase their annual income to the extent of Rs. 13,400. Similarly, in Puri district the mean annual household income of the dairy and non-diary households is estimated at Rs. 54,800 and Rs. 39,500 respectively. The difference of mean income between dairy and non-dairy households is to the extent of Rs. 15,300, which is attributed to the marginal changes in annual households' income due to dairying. Thus, the influence of dairying on the mean changes in household income is found better in Puri district. The overall mean income of all households in Ganjam district is lagging behind Puri district by an amount of Rs. 1,500.

Among all sample households in Ganjam district majority of the members of sample households, 42 per cent have their educational qualification up to secondary level followed by primary (23.08), higher secondary (20.17%) and above higher secondary (8.32). The proportionate share of illiterate people is found lowest.

The mean years of schooling among household members in Ganjam is calculated at 8.28 which are 8.56 among the dairy households and 7.82 among non-dairy households. Perhaps, due to increased income arising out of dairying, the access to education is better availed among the dairy households. In Puri district, the overall mean years of schooling are estimated at 7.33, which is 6.89 among the dairy households and 6.56 among the non-diary households.

It is revealed that 83.7 per cent of dairy households are having television which is only 219 in non-dairy households in Ganjam district. As against 52.1 per cent own watches, only 9.8 per cent of non-dairy households own watches. Similarly, the incidence of motor cycle, pressure cooker, steel furniture, dug wells etc. among dairy households are mostly reported. On the basis of asset holding details, it is fair enough to say that dairy households command more entitlement than non-dairy households. Equally Puri district marks the same trend.

It is revealed that 48 per cent of the households have a Bank deposit, 29 per cent of households have post office deposits, 24 per cent of households have LIC policies, 15% households have some form of bonds/debentures and 4 per cent households have company shares/securities in Ganjam district. On other hand 16 per cent of the households have bank deposits and the 7% of the households have LIC policies in Puri district.

In comparison to non-dairy households, dairy household excel more in all type of deposits. Even bonds, debentures, shares/securities which are not found among non-dairy households, which are reported among dairy households in both the districts under the study.

In Ganjam, among dairy households, almost 32 per cent of the households have bank account which is only 16 per cent in the case of non-dairy households. Similarly, 21 per cent dairy households own LIC polices which are only 30 for non dairy households. Similarly as against 2 per cent of households own postal deposits among non-dairy households, it is more than 13 times higher among non-dairy households. Similarly, in Puri district, 37 per cent of the dairy households have post-office deposit as against 21 per cent among the non-dairy households. In other financial aspects also dairy households are better equipped than the non-dairy households. From this analysis it follows that dairy households have significantly better financial assets than dairy households.

The housing characteristics of dairy households are better than non-dairy households.

In Puri district, the average amount of loan borrowed by dairying households is higher then their counterparts in Ganjam district except as in case of Regional Rural Banks (RRBs). In the non-dairying households also the average amount borrowed from commercial banks and regional rural banks in Ganjam is higher than their counterparts in Puri district.

Around 90 per cent of the sample households are having more than 2 living rooms inside their houses in both the districts. Around 73 per cent of the households have separate cowsheds, around 75 per cent of the households have separate kitchens in their houses, around 45 per cent of the households use non-traditional chullahas like bio-gas and LPG stoves; more than 60 per cent of the households have access to safe drinking water (tube-well water and tap water) and around 52 per cent of the households have access to latrine facility.

The mean PCPDC of all households in Ganjam stands at 634 grams as against the overall mean PCP CD 650.2 in Puri District It is found that the mean PCPDC of dairy households is 649 grams as against 610 grams in Ganjam. On the other hand, the mean PCPDC for dairy and non-dairy households is found at 618 and 635 respectively. The mean PCPDC of cereals of dairy households is slightly higher than the non-dairy households in both the districts.

The PCPDC of pulses among dairy households stands at 660.00 grams as against 51.9 gms among non-dairy households. In Ganjam, the mean PCPDC of pulses of dairy households is 74.5 grams which is found lower at 57.5 grams among non-dairy households. Similarly, the mean PCPDC of pulses of among dairy households and non-dairy households in Puri district is found to be at 60.0 and 41.8 respectively.

It is further evident that the mean PCPDC of dairy as well as non-dairy households in Ganjam is better than the corresponding categories of households in Puri district.

In order to explain the consumption pattern of other food items, the mean monthly per capita consumption expenditure (MPCE) other food items is separately calculated for dairy and non-dairy households in both the districts under study. From the statement given in Table 7.3, it is revealed that the MPCE on meat, fish of dairy household are higher than the corresponding values of non-dairy households by 122.83 per cent and 44.97 per cent respectively in Ganjam district. However, the consumption pattern of egg is slightly lower among dairy households. There has been 223.89 per cent increase in milk consumption among dairy households. It is reported that some of the dairy households have substituted milk for egg. There is negligible difference in the consumption of vegetable. However there is significant difference in the consumption pattern of fruits, confectionary processed foods and biscuits. These increased in the consumption pattern of other food items are attributed to higher income of the dairy households.

In Puri district, the mean MPCE on meat and fish among dairy households are higher to the extent of 116.90 and 13.29

respectively. The decrease in MPCE on egg of dairy household is to the extent 31.30 per cent. The consumption pattern for milk and milk products among diary households is found higher to the extent 31.30 per cent.

In Ganjam district, there has been more than 300 per cent increase in MPCE of dairy households in the items like telephone, entertainment, travel, toiletry and cosmetics. Similarly, for the times like hotel/teas hop and footwear, etc. 200-300 per cent increase in MPCE is reported among the dairy households. More than 100 per cent increase but less than 200 per cent increase is found in MPCE on clothing fuel, medical expenses and education expenses of the dairy households. Around 97 per cent increase in MPCE on newspapers, periodicals is observed among dairy households. There is not much difference in the use of intoxicants, *pan, beedi* and cigarettes etc., among both types of households.

Due to increased income, the dairy households are able to spend more on entertainment, health/education and other luxurious consumption. Due to dairy activity, there have been eye-catching changes in the consumption pattern of rural households, which is a positive sign of rural development.

In Puri district, the highest increase is reported on entertainment and telephone among the dairy households. Increased MPCE to the extent of 200-300 per cent is found for the items like toiletry, and cosmetics. MPCE on the items like intoxicants, *pan, beedi* and cigarettes is found to be declining among dairy households. Similarly, on education, there has been an appreciable change among the dairy households which is also better than Ganj am district. On the basis of analysis of MPCE on non-food items it is revealed that in Puri district, due to diary activities, there has been increased access to telephone, education, newspapers, lower consumption of intoxicants etc. Again increased spending on entertainment, toiletry, and cosmetic indicate the urban bias of rural households. In this background, the impact of diary and rural development is encouraged which are found the study of dairy household in both the districts.

It is found that found per cent of the dairy households and 13 per cent of the non-dairy households in Ganjam are having PCPDC with less than 2400 calories. These households are identified as the households affected by food poverty. Similarly, in Puri district two per cent of the dairy households and around nine per cent of the non-dairy households are affected by food poverty in both the districts. Among all sample households around 6.8 per cent of the households are said to be affected by food poverty. As per our analysis, there are 1.5 per cent of the dairy households and 5 per cent of the non-dairy households in both the districts under study are found with calories' shortfall or food poverty affected households.

It is found that among dairy households in Ganjam district, enrolment ratio has increased by 15 per cent and dropout rate is reduced by around 83 per cent. There has been increased access to latrine and safe drinking water by 34.66 per cent and 15.57 per cent respectively. Similarly, in Puri district enrolment ratio has increased by 12 per cent and drop out ratio is declined by 56.14 per cent. Marginal access to and safe drinking waters is reported to be around 41 per cent and 13.21 per cent respectively. Thus, it is viewed that dairying activity in rural areas are also influencing the key parameters associated with human development, which is a part of the rural development.

## OBSERVATIONS

The bovine stock of the sample households which consists of bullock, non-descript cows, crossbred cows/calves, buffaloes/ calves, goats/and sheep. Thc mean stock of crossbred cows is marginally higher in Puri district.

Among dairy households the mean holding animal is found highest among small farmers followed by large farmers and others in Ganjam district. On the other hand, marginal farmers dominate so far as livestock possession is concerned.

Around 35 per cent of the dairy households supply their milk to primary milk producers cooperative, 38 per cent of the households supply their milk to vendor and the rest 37 per cent to the consumers in Ganjam district. Many a times the dairy farmers are discouraged by the cooperatives on false pleas of bad quality milk and the payment is not instantaneous. Similarly, middlemen offer lower price, which is around 30 per cent less than the market price.

About 41 per cent of farmers keep their cows solely under stall feeding conditions and 32 per cent of the farmers are feeding adequate amount of green fodder to their animals in sample area and the use of green-fodder is more during rainy season.

The mean AFC for non-descript cows between dairying households of Puri and Ganjam is found significant at 5 per cent level of significance (3.959) for other animals the mean AFC is not significant. However, for all animals there is a significant difference between AFC in Ganjam and Puri districts (4.302).

Except buffaloes there is no significance difference between mean lactation length of the milch animals in Ganjam and Puri. The mean lactation length for buffaloes is significant because the t-value is found at 3.690 at 5 per cent level of significance.

The mean milking period for all type of milch animals stands higher in Puri district. Employment and feed intake on the dairy group as compared to the non-dairy group obviously demonstrate the wholesome impact of the HCDP on these parameters in the study area.

The independent variables included in the regression equation explained 72 to 82 per cent of the variation in milk production being maximum non-descript cows and minimum in local buffaloes on the non-dairy households. Among the different inputs, the regression coefficients of green fodder and concentrates were positive and highly significant in all the equations fitted. The concentrate was the most important variable which had significant and positive regression coefficient in all the equations. On the dairy households the regression coefficient of concentrates was maximum in the case of nondescript cows (0.1506) and minimum in the case of cross-bred cows (0.0932) while in the case of non-beneficiaries, the regression coefficient of this input was maximum in the case of non-descript cows (0.1734) and minimum in the case of local buffaloes (0.1724). It shows that the concentrate was the most important factor affecting the milk production in all the breeds of cows and buffaloes both on the dairy and non-dairy households.

The regression coefficient of green fodder on the dairy households was minimum for graded buffaloes (0.0813) and maximum for cross-bred cows (0.1063), whereas in the case of non-beneficiaries, the regression coefficient of this input was minimum for nondescript cows (0.0888) and maximum for local buffaloes (0.0896), showing the corresponding percentage increase in value of milk due to one rupee increase in expenditure on green fodder. Though the regression coefficient of dry fodder was positive it was not statistically significant in all the regression equations fitted, except for crossbred cows on the dairy households. The reason for non-significant regression coefficients of dry fodder can be described to the lack of variation in the quantity of dry fodder.

The regression coefficient of labour was significant only in the case of graded buffaloes and order of lactation was significant in the case of local buffaloes only. The regression coefficient of stage of lactation was negative and statistically significant for all the equations on both the groups.

The various factors influencing milk production included in the production functions explained about 62 to 91 per cent of the total variation in milk production in the case of dairy households whereas on the non-dairy group these variables explained about 74 to 80 per cent of the variation.

Green fodder, dry fodder and concentrates were the important inputs in influencing milk production having significant regression coefficients. The coefficient of green fodder was significant and positive for all the breeds of cows and buffaloes on both the dairy and non-dairy groups except for non-descript cows on the non-dairy group.

Miscellaneous expenditure had uniformly poor influence on the non-dairy households and graded buffaloes due to lack of variation in the variable itself and also due to the low degree of engagement.

Milk production registers an increase in all breeds with an increase in green fodder at their mean levels. The dry fodder had a significantly positive impact on milk production only for non-descript cows and graded buffaloes on the dairy group.

Per day sale proceeds and operating expenses for non-descript cows are estimated at 6.20 and 4.21 respectively in Ganjam district. Thus, net-income per non-descript cows is found at Rs. 1.99. This figure is further lower in Puri district, where sale proceeds and operating expenses per milch animals are Rs. 6041 and Rs. 4.90 respectively.

It is observed that there is not much difference in the net income for all types of milch animals in the districts under study.

It is inferred from the analysis that landless labourers are also reported in dairy activity. Due to the lack of on-farm and off-farm employment opportunities in rural areas, most often landless people pursue dairying as a promising economic activity.

Around 50 per cent of the households engaged in dairying are not able to get sufficient employment opportunities in the existing scale of their respective dairying. There is further scope of increasing milk production even among the dairy households. Further, the non-workers can also be motivated towards dairying.

The difference of mean income between dairy and non-dairy households is to the extent of Rs. 15,300, which is attributed to the marginal changes in annual households' income due to dairying. Thus, the influence of dairying on the mean changes in household income is found better in Puri district. The overall mean income of all households in Ganjam district is lagging behind Puri district by an amount of Rs. 1,500.

Due to increased income arising out of dairying, the access to education is better availed among the dairy households.

On the basis of asset holding details, it is fair enough to say that dairy households command more entitlement than non-dairy households. Dairy households have significantly better financial assets than dairy households.

Households have been able to increase their annual income. The difference of mean income between dairy and non-dairy households is to the extent of Rs. 15,300, which is attributed to the marginal changes in annual households' income due to dairying. Due to increased income arising out of dairying, the access to education is better availed among the dairy households. It is fair enough to say that dairy households command more entitlement than non-dairy households. Dairy households have significantly better financial assets than dairy households. The housing characteristics of dairy households are better than non-dairy households.

In Puri district, the average amount of loan borrowed by dairying households is higher then their counterparts in Ganjam district except as in case of Regional Rural Banks (RRBs). In the non-dairying households also the average amount borrowed from commercial banks and regional rural banks in Ganjam is higher than their counterparts in Puri district.

The mean PCPDC of cereals of dairy households is slightly higher than the nondairy households in both the districts.

The mean PCPDC of pulses of among dairy households and non-dairy households in Puri district is found to be at 60.0 and 41.8 respectively. These increased in the consumption pattern of other food items are attributed to higher income of the dairy households. The consumption pattern for milk and milk products among diary households is found higher to the extent 31.30 per cent. There is not much difference in the use of intoxicants, *pan, beedi* and cigarettes etc. among both types of households.

Due to increased income, the dairy households are able to spend more on entertainment, health / education and other luxurious consumption. Due to dairy activity, there have been eye-catching changes in the consumption pattern of rural households, which is a positive sign of rural development.

Increased spending on entertainment, toiletry, and cosmetic indicate the urban bias of rural households. In this background, the impact of diary and rural development is encouraged which are found the study of dairy household in both the districts.

It is viewed that dairying activity in rural areas are also influencing the key parameters associated with human development, which is a part of the rural development.

## SUGGESTIONS

On the basis of the above averments, it is felt that the dairy sector in the Orissa needs to reorganise and revamp its policies keeping in view of the poor financial performance of the state in dairy sector. Some of the suggestions, which may prove helpful, are laid below.

1. Equipping and empowering the small producers with information and skills to maximise returns, through appropriate technologies and self-help approach to problem solving.
2. Promotion and nurturing of grass root level participatory bodies all over the state, as the organic link between the animal husbandry department and the small holders.
3. Promoting appropriate technologies, enhancing productivity and increasing effectiveness for assured returns.
4. Development and protection of village common land, i.e. pasture and grazing land to facilitate bovine stock for grazing and free movement.
5. Introduction of green fodder cultivation incentives to farmers who cultivate it for at least five years.
6. Intensification of cross-breeding programme through artificial insemination, technology for production of genetically superior cattle and buffaloes.
7. Devising ways to ensure the sectoral growth with the active and gainful participation of the resource poor throughout the state through commercial credit,

concessional and liberalised credit scheme, and increased subsidy on dairy entrepreneurship.

8. Ensuring more and more participation of women and weaker section of people from the community level.
9. Government resolution in regard to disease control of the bovine stock and quality control mechanism in the dairy sector.
10. Restructuring and revitalising existing institutional set up in the livestock sector, and enhancing institution level efficiency and promote new institutional models to handle the emerging challenges in sector development.
11. Strengthening the level of knowledge of the farmers on dairy management, breeding and feeding through training, awareness and orientation programme.

## POINTERS FOR FURTHER RESEARCH

Orissa, one of the most backward states in the dairy scenario in the country has been drawing the focus of planners and policy-makers for its unique failure to take advantage of the dairy development programme to ameliorate the economic conditions of the rural poor. As the study of different aspects of contribution of dairying and its impact in the State at micro level would be helpful to administrators in analysing the dismal performance of the sector so that proper remedial measures could be designed to augment and sustain the dairy development and in turn, rural development in the State. Though the present research has identified the merits associated with dairying in the sphere of rural development, there is much scope for expanding dairying base in the rural areas through better penetration of genetic engineering, infrastructure development, and better access to finance.

# Bibliography


Attwood, D.W., and Baviskar, B.S. (1993), "Introduction". In: *Cooperatives and Rural Development*, Oxford University Press, Delhi.

Alvares, Claude (1985), Imperialism through Food Aid: The Role of Third World Elites: Part-I ed. In: *Another Revolution Fails*, Ajanta Publications, New Delhi.

Alvares, Claude (1985), Operation Flood the White Lies. In: ed. *Another Revolution Fails*, Ajanta Publications, New Delhi.

Andrews, Frederick N. (1967), *Artificial Insemination: It's Role on Livestock Improvement*, Forum Lecturers-Agriculture, U.S.A. Government Publications.

Apte, D.P. (1993), The Role of Cooperative Dairy Schemes in Rural Development in India, In: Attwood and Baviskar (eds.), *Who Shares Cooperatives and Rural Development*, Oxford University Press.

Baumal, Willam J. (1973), *Economic Theory and Operational Analysis*, Prentice-Hall of India Private Ltd.

Baviskar, B.S. (1994), "Dairy cooperatives and Rural Development in Gujarat" In: Attwood and Baviskar (eds.), *Who Shares Cooperatives and Rural Development*, Oxford University Press.

Baviskar, B.S. (1990), "Dairy Cooperatives and Rural Development in Gujarat", In: Doornbos, M and Nair, K.N. Eds.), *Resources, Institutions and Strategies: Operation Flood and Indian Dairying*, Sage Publications, New Delhi.

Bhanja, S.K. and Venkatadri, S. (1988), *Milch Cattle in Integrated Rural Development Programme*, NIRD, Hyderabad.

Bowander, B., Dasgupta, B., Gupta, S. and Prasad, S.S.R. (1987), "Further Evidence on the impact of Dairy Development, *Economic and Political Weekly*, March p. A-15.

Brundaban, Samal (1988), *A Short History of Veterinary Medicine and Animal Husbandry in Orissa*, Panchashilla Publications, Bhubaneswar.

Candler, W. and N. (1998) India: The Diary Revolution, The Impact of Dairy Development in India and the World Bank Contribution, The World Bank, Washington, D.C.

Devendra, C. (1981), Socio-Economic Importance of Goat Production, In: Gall, (ed), *Goat Production*, Academic Press, London.

Dhebar, U.N. (1967), *Khadi Gramodyog*, Dec.

Dogra Bharat (1985), "Economics and Politics of Food-Aid, In: Alvares and Kotahri (eds.), *Another Revolution Fails*, Ajanta Publications, New Delhi.

Dogra, Bharat (1985), Economics and Politics and Food aid Part-II In: Alvares, Claude (ed.), *Another Revolution Fails*, Ajanta Publications, New Delhi.

Doomboas, M., Frank Van Dorsrten, Monoshi Mitra and Pietehral (1987), *Assessing Dairy Development: Towards a Research Approach to India's Operation Flood*, Netherlands Review of Development Studies.

Dorsten, F. Van (1986), *Operation Flood : The EEC Connection*, ISS/IDPAD Working Paper. No. 18, Dairy Aid and Development.

Dutt, Ruddar, (1997), *Organising the Unorganized Workers*, Vikas Publishing House, New Delhi.

Food and Agricultural Organisation J. (1999), *Global Food Outlook Report*, Rome.

Gearge, P.S. and Srivastava; U.K. (1975) "Institutional Finance for Dairy Development" *Indian Journal of Agricultural Economics*, Vol. XXX (3) July-Sept., pp. 90-96.

George, Shanti J. (1993), Cooperatives and Indian Dairy Policy: More Anand than Pattern in Attwood and Baviskar B.S. (ed.) *Cooperatives and Rural Development*, Oxford University Press, Delhi.

George, Shanti (1985), *Operation Flood: An Appraisal of Current Indian Dairy Policy*, Oxford University Press, New Delhi.

Goswami, S.N. and Rao N.V. (1992), Economics of Milk Production in the East Khasi Hills Districts, *Indian Journal of Dairy Science*, Vol. 45, No. 2.

Government of India (1976), *Report of National Commission on Agriculture*, 1976.

Government of India (2001), About NDDB.

Government of India (2001), *Annual Report 2000-01*, Department of Animal Husbandry and Dairying, Ministry of Agriculture.

Government of India (GOI), 2001, *National Accounts Statistics-2001*, Central Statistical Organisation.

Government of India (2004), Basic Animal Husbandry Statistics, Ministry of Agriculture, Government of India, New Delhi.

Government of India (2004); Department of Animal Husbandry and Dairying, Ministry of Agriculture, New Delhi, http:/www.dahd.nic.in/tabs.

Government of Orissa (1990), *Economic Survey (1989-90)*, Directorate of Economics and Statistics, Planning & Coordination Department .

Government of Orissa (1991), *Economic Survey (1990-91)*, Directorate of Economics and Statistics, Planning & Coordination Department.

Government of Orissa (1992), *Economic Survey (1991-92)*, Directorate of Economics and Statistics, Planning & Coordination Department.

Government of Orissa (1993), *Economic Survey (1992-93)*, Directorate of Economics and Statistics, Planning & Coordination Department.

Government of Orissa (1994), *Economic Survey (1993-94)*, Directorate of Economics and Statistics, Planning & Coordination Department.

Government of Orissa (1995), *Economic Survey (1994-95)*, Directorate of Economics and Statistics, Planning & Coordination Department.

Government of Orissa (1996), *Economic Survey (1995-96)*, Directorate of Economics and Statistics, Planning & Coordination Department.

Government of Orissa (2000), *Economic Survey (1999-2000)*, Directorate of Economics and Statistics, Planning & Coordination Department.

Government of Orissa (2001), *Economic Survey (2000-01)*, Directorate of Economics and Statistics, Planning & Coordination Department.

Government of Orissa (2002), *Economic Survey (2002-03)*, Directorate of Economics and Statistics, Planning & Coordination Department.

Gupta, J.N. and Kumar P. (1988), Resource Use Efficiency in Milk Production in Muzzaffar Nagar district of Uttar Pradesh, *Asian Journal of Dairy Research,* Vol. 7, No. 4.

Gupta P.R. (1987), *Dairy in India*, Rekha Printers Private Ltd., New Delhi.

Gunnar, Myrdall (1989), Aims of Planning, In: Madan, G.R. (ed), *Economic Problems of Modern India: Problems of Development*, Allied Publications, Bombay.

Heredero, J.M. (1992), "Milk Co-operatives and Tribal Poverty in Gujarat: The need of education and Management", in

*National Development and Tribal Deprivation*, Edited by Walter Fernandes, Indian Social Institute, New Delhi, pp. 285-315.

Huria, Vinod K. and Acharya, K.T. (1980) Dairy development in India: Some Critical Issues, *Economic and Political Weekly*, Vol. XV (45&46) Nov. 8-15 pp. 1931-1942

Jain, Sugan Chand (1979) "Dairying in India" in Southern Economist, February.

Jayachandra, K. (1991), *Cost Management in Dairy Industry*, Discovery Publishing House, New Delhi.

Kahlon, A.S., Dhawan, K.C. and Gill, G.S. (1975), Relative profitability of Dairy Enterprise *vis-a-vis* Crop cultivation in the Punjabi *Indian Journal of Agricultural Economics*, Vol. XXX(3), pp. 120-128.

Kherde, R.L. and Subramaniam, R. (1980) "Impact of Milk marketing through Dairy cooperative; The Indian Dairy Man, V 01.38 (8) August p. 404.

Korten, D.C. (1981), Rural Development Programming, The learning Process Approach, pp. 1-8, Rural Development Committee, Winter 1981, *Rural Development Participation Review* 2 , Ithaca, NY, U.S.A., Cornell University.

Madan Mohan, C., (1989), *Dairy Management in India: A study in Andhra Pradesh*, Mittal Publications, Delhi.

Mishra, S.N. and Shanna, Rishi. K. (1990), *Livestock Development in India: An Appraisal*, Vikàs Publishing House, New Delhi.

Naik D. and Mohanty B.C. (1995), Economics of Milk Production with Special Reference to Resource Use in the Existing Market Environment of Orissa, Indian Journal of Agricultural Economics, Vol. 50, No. 3.

Nair, K.N. (1982), "Technological Change in Milk Production: A Review of some Critical Issues with Reference to South Asia", *Economic and Political Weekly*, Vol. 17, no. B.

National Dairy Development Board (2003): *About NDDB, Government of India*, New Delhi.

NDDB (1976), *A Report on Operation Flood: Success Story*, The World's Biggest Dairy Development Programme.

NDDB (1979), Operation Flood, Government of India , New Delhi.

Oberai, A.S., Sivananthiran, A.. and Venkata Ratnam, C.S., (2000), *Perspectives on Unorganised Labour*, edited by, ILO, IIRA, New Delhi, ILO, New Delhi.

OMFED: Various Issues of Annual Reports and Souvenirs upto 2004.

Pandey, R.N., Bhogal, T.S. and Verma; M.L. (1975), Economic Impact of Dairy Development Project, Aligarh, *Indian Journal of Agricultural Economics*. Vol. XXX(3), pp. 158-159.

Parida, Bhagyarathi (2009), Orissa Milk Federation launches low-fat skimmed milk, *Orissa Business News*.

Patel, A.S. (1993), "Cooperative Dairying and Rural Development: A Case study of AMUL, In: Attwood and Baviskar B.S. (eds.), *Cooperatives and Rural Development*, Oxford University Press, Delhi.

Patel, V.M. (1987) "Impact of Milk Co-operatives in Gujarat" *Indian Dairyman*, Vol. 39(6), June, pp. 293-96.

Phukan, Umananda and Goshain, Debasish (1975) "Dairy farming in the Brahmaputra Valley of Assam: A case study: *Indian Journal of Agricultural Economics*, Vol. XXX(3), p. 160.

Radha Krishnan, S.A, and Singnandham, M. (1975), Dairying as a subsidiary enterprise in Farms—A micro level analysis, *Indian Journal of Agricultural Economics*, Vol. XXX (3).

Report of the *National Commission on Agriculture* 1976, Vol. VII-Animal Husbandry, Government of India, Ministry of Agriculture and Irrigation, New Delhi, p. 1.

Sah Abhaya and Srivastava, U.K. (1985), *Rice bran Oil Industry: An Insight into Technology and Commercial Aspects*. Concept Publishing House, New Delhi.

Savara, M. (1990), "Dairy Development Amongst the Tribals in Surat District", Resources, Institutions and Strategies Operation Flood and Indian Dairying, Darnabas, M and Nair, K.N. (ed.) p. 247-299.

Shah, Dillip R. (1992), *Dairy Co-operativization: An Instrument of Social Change*, Rawat Publications, Jaipur.

Sharma, Vijaya Paul and Singh, Raj Vir (1993), 'Resource Productivity and Allocation Efficiency in Milk Production in Himachal Pradesh', *Indian Journal of Agricultural Economics*, vol. 48 (2), April-June, pp. 201-215.

Singh, Daroga, Murthy, V.V.R. and Goel B.B.P.S. (1970), *Monograph on Estimation of Milk Production*, New Delhi, lARS, ICAR.

Singh, J.P., Chakravarty, M.L. and Das R.N. (1995), Factors influencing Milk Production: A Study in Khurda Block of Khurda District (Orissa), *Indian Journal of Agricultural Economics*, Vol. 50, No. 3.

Singh, K and Das, V.M. (1980), "Impact of Operational Flood - I at village level, (Memeo), Institute of Rural Management, Anand. pp. 2-5.

Singh, M. Verma, D.S. and Yadava, S.P. (1985), Analysis of Operational Efficiency Structure of U.P Milk Co-operatives in *Indian Co-operative Review,* Vol. 22 (4), August, p. 397.

Sixth Five year Plan, 1980-85, Andhra Pradesh, Draft Finance and Planning Commission, GoAP, Hyderabad, 1980, vol. II, p. 63.

Srivastava UK (1989); Agro Processing Industries, Potential constraints and task ahead, *Indian Journal of Agriculture Economics*, Vol. XLIV (3).

Thakur, D.S. (1975), Impact of Dairy Development through Milk co-operatives A Case Study of Gujarat. *Indian Journal of Agricultural Economics*, Vol. XXX (3) July-Sept pp. 83-89.

Thirunavukkarasu, M., Pravbaharan, R and Ramaswamy, (1991) "Impact of operation Flood on the income and employment of Rural poor-Some Micro level Evidences" *Journal of Rural Development*, Vol. 10(4) pp. 417-425, NIRD Hyderabad.

Thomas, C.A. (1974), No White Revolution without Green Revolution, in Yojana, January.

Vaidyanathan, A. (1988), *Bovine Economy in India*, Centre for Development Studies, monograph series, Oxford and IBH Publication, Private Ltd. New Delhi.

Venkatasubramanian, V. (1991), Training of Rural Women in Dairying for Rural Development, Khadi Grammodyog, VoI. 36, No. 8.

Verhagen, M. (1990), "Operation Flood and the Rural Poor" In: Doornbos and Nair, KN. (eds.), *Resources, Institutions and Strategies, Operational Flood and Indian Dairying*, Sage Publications, New Delhi, pp. 229-255.

Whyte, R.O. and Mathur M.L. (1968), *The Planning of Milk Production*, Orient Longman, New Delhi.

# Index


**A**

Acharya 25

Age at first calving 103

AI services 59

Amul and the evolution of the Anand model 9

Ananda pattern dairy co-operative structure 36

Andhra Pradesh 32

Artificial insemination 29

Atibudhi 36

**B**

Baviskar, B.S. 33

Bawander, B. 31

**C**

Common property resources 101

Communicable disease 29

Concentrates 27, 31, 103, 114

Constraints in dairy development 112

Crossbred cows 23, 38, 84, 115, 114, 117

**D**

Dairy and non-dairy households 16

Dairy development in Orissa 40

Dairying 18

Dairying prior to operation flood 7

Definitions used 16

Dry fodder 27, 31, 114, 102

**E**

Economics of dairying among the sample households 84

**F**

Feeding practices 103

Fuel used for cooking 77

**G**

Garg 22

George 21

Goshain 20

Green fodder 27, 114, 101

Gujarat 21, 35

**H**

Haryana 24

Heredero, J.M. 35

**I**

Impact of dairying on rural development 144

Independent Sleeping Rooms 76
Introduction 1-19

**K**

Kahlon 22
Kkarasu, Thirunavu 34
Krishnan, Radha 22

**L**

Lactation length 104
Lactation number 104
Landholding pattern 119
Landless labourers 13

**M**

Madan Mohan, C. 32
Madhya Pradesh 37
Manbhekar 37
Milch animals 104
Milking Period 107
Milk-marketing process 117

**N**

National Dairy Research Institute, Karnal 38
Non-dairy households 130, 150
Non-descript cows 84, 101, 113, 114, 115, 117

**O**

Operation flood 12, 25, 32, 51, 55
Orissa women's dairy project 63
Overall 115

**P**

Paddy straw 102
Pandey 21, 27
Patel, V.M. 31
Pattern of Drinking Water 76
Phase I (1970-1980) 11
Phase II (1981-85) 11
Phase III (1985-1996) 12
Profile of the Study Area 65
Punjab 22

**R**

Rainy season 113
Ram 25
Rao 23
Raut 23
Reddy 23, 24
Reference period 18
Rekib 24, 31
Review of literature 20-3

**S**

Sanitation 77
Savara, M. 33
Scheduled Caste 13, 34
Scheduled Tribes 13, 34
Scheme of the study 18
Selection of blocks and villages 15
Selection of districts 15
Selection of respondents 16
Shah, D.R. 35
Singh, K. 25
Singh, M. 29
Socio-economic status of the sample households 118
Source of lighting 77
Statistical techniques Used 19
Statistical tools used 19
Summer season 112

**T**

Tamil Nadu 22, 34

Thakur, D.S. 21

Tribal poverty 35

Type of housing 135

**U**

U.P milk co-operatives 29

Ultra high temperature (UHT) treatment 26

Uttar Pradesh 22

**V**

Vashist 32

Verhagen, M. 32

Winter Season 114

**Z**

Zebu cows 38

❑❑❑